Territorial Seas and Inter-American Relations

Bobbie B. Smetherman
Robert M. Smetherman

The Praeger Special Studies program—
utilizing the most modern and efficient book
production techniques and a selective
worldwide distribution network—makes
available to the academic, government, and
business communities significant, timely
research in U.S. and international economic, social, and political development.

Territorial Seas and Inter-American Relations

With Case Studies of the Peruvian and U.S. Fishing Industries

PRAEGER SPECIAL STUDIES IN INTERNATIONAL POLITICS AND GOVERNMENT

Praeger Publishers New York Washington London

Library of Congress Cataloging in Publication Data

Smetherman, Bobbie B
    Territorial seas and inter-American relations.

    (Praeger special studies in international politics
and government)
    Includes bibliographical references.
    1. Territorial waters—Peru. 2. United States—
Foreign relations—Latin America. 3. Latin America—
Foreign relations—United States. 4. Fisheries—
United States. 5. Fisheries—Peru. I. Smetherman,
Robert M., joint author. II. Title.
JX4131.S53   341.44'8   74-6734
ISBN 0-275-08900-2

PRAEGER PUBLISHERS
111 Fourth Avenue, New York, N.Y. 10003, U.S.A.
5, Cromwell Place, London SW7 2JL, England

Published in the United States of America in 1974
by Praeger Publishers, Inc.

Printed in the United States of America

CONTENTS

Territorial Seas and
Inter-American Relations

One of the most persistent and seemingly insolvable problems of postwar inter-American relations has been the dispute over boundaries for territorial waters. Ten Latin American nations now claim either a "territorial sea" or some special maritime zone extending 200 miles offshore. Unless the United Nations can write a universally accepted international treaty on the law of the sea, the number of claimants is likely to grow, both in this hemisphere and elsewhere. The ten countries maintain their claims in contradiction to the traditional law of the sea and the wishes of the world's major maritime nations, especially the United States. The subject is complex and multifaceted. The political and economic issues provoked by the multiple uses of the oceans are not only knotty but also overlapping, labyrinthine, and frequently anomalous. We hope that this study will illuminate some of the complexity.

One theme that lies at the heart of the dispute over territorial waters concerns the development process in various countries. The extension claim, in addition to the intermittent efforts of some of the claimants to enforce and spread their claims, indicate a chronic struggle involving the goals of developing coastal nations and those of developed maritime nations. At the very least, the claimants hope to reduce the likelihood that the world's developed maritime nations will drain the hemisphere of valuable natural resources in an offshore "colonial" or "imperialist" exploitation. In this instance the traditional concept of "freedom of the seas" has been defined by the Latin American nations as a kind of marine colonialism. They are convinced that U.S. opposition to the 200-mile claim is a transparent exercise in dollar diplomacy. The United States has only two distant-water fisheries--

tuna and shrimp. Both are high-value fisheries operating
in waters off the coasts of Latin American nations.

The claim and the defense of it, both diplomatically
and physically, have become important to the claiming nations as a means of asserting and achieving a certain degree of independence in foreign policy. This study ex-
plores the relationship between independence and interdependence of nations and shows that sometimes the distinction between the two is somewhat illusory. Investigation
of this subject provides a very interesting excursion into
the group nature of politics, especially the influence of
domestic interest groups on a nation's foreign policy, frequently provoking retaliatory responses from other nations.
Nationalism is a very important component of the claim,
sometimes revealing more about domestic political power
and instabilities than about foreign policy absolutes.
The 200-mile claim has become a shibboleth for the Latin
American claimants and sympathizers, as well as for a number of Third World imitators outside the hemisphere. It
is a distinctive feature of their national pride and increasing national independence; they make symbolic use of
the claims, of boat seizures and the imposition of heavy
fines, and of international lobbying to spread the claim,
and substantiate the fact that they are achieving greater
national independence.

Another recurrent theme of this study is the nature
of fisheries--their ownership, competition, and conservation. The conservation of fish stocks is all too often
embodied in a demand by those who got there first to keep
latecomers from competing in the fishery. The demands of
a nation's fishing industry for international conservation
frequently disguise its desire for exclusive, or nearly
exclusive, exploitation of the resource. The questions of
ownership of migratory fish stocks pit the interests of
the fishery's discoverers against the claims of adjacent
and other nations.

The phenomenal Peruvian fishmeal boom has stimulated
considerable envy on the part of other Latin American nations and a desire to gain similar profits from oceanic
riches. Even though the other Latin American nations know
that the waters off their coasts are not nearly as bounti-
ful as the fish resources in Peru's Humboldt Current, they
have concluded that whatever fish resources do exist off
their coasts should be developed and exploited under their
control and for their profit. As Chapter 4 details, however, the development of the lucrative Peruvian fishing
industry has not been an unmixed blessing. This fishery

is explored in depth because it is the most highly developed Latin American fishery and also because Peru's position on the 200-mile territorial sea claim has been the most zealous and intransigent position of any claimant.

A variety of other issues involved in the subject are treated in this study, including the origin of the international law of the sea and how it should be changed--that is, can a unilateral extension of territorial seas or of fishing zones be accepted? Other subjects include the economic and biological theories and techniques of fishery management, and the lure of great potential wealth from offshore resources--fish, petroleum, or minerals. The powerful U.S. tuna fishing industry is also analyzed economically and politically, with special emphasis on the impact it has had on the U.S. Congress directly and on Latin American foreign policies indirectly. Another major topic considered here is the difficulties that impede the development of a uniform oceans policy for the world, for the United States, or for any nation for that matter. Multiple uses of the oceans have created conflicting potential and existing needs, interests, and interest groups--both national and multinational. If a satisfactory solution to the problems raised by the 200-mile claim is to be achieved, many of these conflicting viewpoints will have to be compromised for the greater good of achieving a universally accepted international law of the sea.

Chapter 2 traces the history of the claim, the dispute, and the attempts to settle the issue. Chapter 3 deals with the impact of the 200-mile claim on Latin American foreign policy, especially Peruvian and Ecuadorian foreign policy. The impact of the Peruvian fishmeal industry on the Peruvian economy and government is analyzed in detail in Chapter 4. Chapter 5 is an analysis of the economics and political power of the U.S. tuna industry. Chapter 6 presents general conclusions.

2

THE 200-MILE CLAIM
AND INTER-AMERICAN
RELATIONS

During the last 20 years the dispute over the extension of territorial waters off Latin America's Pacific
coast has become increasingly damaging to hemispheric cooperation and goodwill. It has stirred bitter resentment
of U.S. foreign policy, since powerful private U.S. interest groups are seen as manipulators of that policy.

HISTORY OF THE CLAIM

The first voicing of concern by a Latin American nation about control over its coastal waters occurred in the
early days of World War I. A Peruvian delegate to the Pan
American Union presented a memorandum on the rights of
neutrals to prevent hostile actions off their coasts.[1] A
major impetus for the claim was supplied in October 1939
when the foreign ministers of the Organization of American
States (OAS) signed the Declaration of Panama at the be-
hest of the United States. The Declaration of Panama established a defense zone around the hemisphere, which extended in some places as far as 300 miles. During the
same period, when the Japanese were fishing for Alaskan
salmon, President Roosevelt asked for a State Department
study on abrogating the three-mile territorial limit as it
applied to fisheries.[2]
The 200-mile extension is not the only claim to fishing rights that a country has made unilaterally. Paradoxically the United States made such a claim on September
28, 1945, when President Truman issued two unilateral proc-
lamations--one regarding the continental shelf and the
other on fisheries. The proclamation on the continental
shelf, which was spurred by the oil industry, declared the

4

shelf and its minerals adjoining the U.S. coasts to be subject to U.S. control, plainly stipulating, however, that
the waters above the continental shelf were not affected
by the declaration. The proclamation on fisheries stated
the need for fisheries conservation in waters contiguous
to the U.S. coasts and proposed the establishment of conservation zones, regulated jointly, or solely by the United States, depending on whether nationals of other countries traditionally fished in these zones. It also proclaimed that any state had the right to establish such
zones off its shores, "provided that corresponding recognition is given to the fishing interests of the nationals
of the United States which may exist in such areas."[3]

Despite the clear distinctions in the Truman proclamations between the subsurface minerals in the continental
shelf and the waters above the shelf, subsequent actions
by Latin American nations ignored or obscured the distinctions. Just one month after the Truman proclamations,
Mexico's President Avila Camacho claimed his country's
continental shelf as Mexican property, expressly claiming
fishing interests.[4] A few months later the Mexican president reaffirmed his earlier decree by proposing a revision
of Article 27 of the Mexican Constitution stating that the
continental shelf, submarine terraces, and the waters over
them belonged to the Mexican nation.

In 1946 Argentina declared all its waters above the
continental shelf, the "epicontinental sea," to be Argentine territory. Its geographic features have provided Argentina with a continental shelf that extends as far as
500 miles offshore at some points. The Argentine declaration specifically exempted controls over navigation from
the intent of its claim.[5] Parenthetically it should be
noted that after a 1967 dispute with Soviet fishing boats,
Argentina redefined her claim to apply not to the continental shelf but to a more precise, and more easily enforce-
able, sovereignty over a 200-mile area off its coast.[6] In
1972 Argentina restricted fishing in her claim to a maximum of 16 foreign vessels at any one time. The foreign
vessels are allowed a total catch of 70,000 tons and they
may fish only for hake, anchovy, and squid.[7]

Unlike the east coast of Latin America, the west
coast has almost no continental shelf--it ranges between
three and thirty miles and the average width is six miles.[8]
In 1947 Chile became the first nation to claim an extension of its territorial waters in terms of distance--200
miles. Chile's primary concern at that time was the extensive whaling off its coast. There are at least two

explanations for the 200-mile figure. It has been suggested that Chilean authorities believed that 200 miles was as far as the rich Humboldt Current had ever moved out to sea.[9] Another reason for this particular distance was that 200 miles was considered to be the maximum distance from which land-based whalers could fish.[10] At any rate, on June 23, 1947, Chilean President Gabriel Gonzales Videla issued the first 200-mile decree, claiming sovereignty over the continental shelf and over the seas above the shelf, and establishing a fishery protection zone of 200 miles, explicitly exempting freedom of navigation from control. A few weeks later, on August 1, 1947, Peru's President José Luís Bastamante y Rivero issued an almost identical decree, noting the Truman proclamation.[11] Ecuador followed suit soon afterwards.

At Chile's invitation, representatives of Ecuador and Peru met in Santiago in 1952 and signed with Chile a joint treaty declaring the 200-mile maritime zone. This declaration claimed that each nation had sovereignty and jurisdiction not only over the sea for 200 miles adjacent to their mainland coasts, but also over surrounding islands belonging to the nation as well; it exempted navigation from control. Two years later the three nations--sometimes called the CEP nations--strengthened their resolution by amending the Declaration of Santiago, specifying that none of the three would diminish the 200-mile claim without prior consultation and agreement with the other two governments. This "loyalty pact" indicates that the claimants were under considerable pressure from the maritime powers, especially the United States, to revoke their claim. For instance there was a conference in 1953 between U.S. and Ecuadorian representatives, in which Ecuador agreed to issue by radio interim licenses to fish in her territorial waters.[12] This conference served to reinforce the claims; U.S. protests merely heightened the issue. The claimants regarded the Truman proclamations as clear precedents and the U.S. protests about their own claims as hypocritical self-interest. The claimants found reinforcement in numbers and in periodic reiterations of the claim.

A short time later Aristotle Onassis sent his German-based, Panamanian-registered whaling fleet into the extension area to test the will of the Peruvian government in enforcing the claim. Five of the eleven whaling vessels were seized and held until joint fines of $3 million were paid. At least three nations protested these seizures: the United States, on principle; Panama, because the whalers were operating under the Panamanian flag; and Britain, because Lloyd's of London had insured the fleet for 90 percent of the costs of seizures.[13]

The Declaration of Santiago seems a remarkable achievement, because in the beginning there was possibly more suspicion among the CEP nations than comradeship. In fact it was less a matter of creating a pact than avoiding oneupmanship. Chile is traditionally Peru's bitter enemy. Therefore, when Chile first made the 200-mile claim, Peru quickly followed her example. Peru's reaction to her catastrophic defeat at Chile's hands in the War of the Pacific (1879-83) had made her especially sensitive on maritime and naval matters.[14] The Peruvian military apparently finds it easy to justify new appropriations on the grounds that Chile has acquired sophisticated new weapons. This rationale was prominent at the time of Peru's purchase of 16 Mirage jet fighters during the 1967 devaluation crisis.[15] In the light of this sort of traditional apprehension it is not surprising that Peru would claim its own extension or even form an uneasy alliance to defend it.

The same pattern of bitter resentment and fear produced by past military defeats at the hands of its neighbor has characterized Ecuador's attitude toward Peru, but to a greater degree. In 1941 the interminable Ecuadorian-Peruvian boundary dispute broke out in open warfare with Peru's superior army and air force quickly routing Ecuador's hapless defenders. The Protocol of Rio de Janeiro, redrawing the boundary between the two nations, was accepted by the Ecuadorian government because it had no choice but to accept it. However, the issue remained a volatile one in Ecuadorian politics, since Ecuador lost about two-thirds of the Oriente that she had claimed as well as access to the Amazon and the Atlantic. Denunciation of the protocol became a standard part of Ecuador's domestic politics, particularly under the flamboyant leadership of its perennial president, Velasco Ibarra. He called the protocol an imposition rather than a treaty, and declared it invalid in 1960. On the anniversary of the signing of the protocol the Ecuadorian government stages protest demonstrations.

The tensions created by the Ecuador-Peru boundary dispute contributed to repeated postponements of the Eleventh Inter-American Conference, which was scheduled to be held in Quito in 1959 but which was never held. This underscores the uneasiness of the CEP partnership; any response to Peruvian leadership in this realm or any other is permeated with a basic distrust.[16]

However, it should be added that a recent study of the Ecuadorian's image of Peru discovered that the hatred and fear has diminished. Ecuadorian political leaders attributed this improved image to several factors, including the joint Ecuadorian and Peruvian defense of the 200-mile claim.[17]

OTHER CLAIMANTS

In the late 1940s and early 1950s several other Latin American nations took action either on the continental shelf concept or the territorial waters concept. Panama's 1946 constitution claimed ownership of the continental shelf and a presidential decree in 1946 established Panamanian jurisdiction over fisheries above the continental shelf. In 1967 the Panamanian National Assembly passed legislation extending the nation's territorial waters 200 miles. Proponents of the measure urged that the maximum fine for encroachment be increased from $10,000 to $100,000 in order to support the additional cost of enforcement.[18]

In 1948 Costa Rica declared a conservation zone for mineral and fish resources for a distance of 200 miles from Costa Rican coasts. In 1966 the Costa Rican President, José Joaquín Trejos Fernandez, under strong pressure from the United States, vetoed a national assembly measure ratifying Costa Rica's adherence to the Declaration of Santiago. For technical, legalistic reasons the legislative proposal was ineffectual; it was a sham, probably designed to upset the United States and put the Costa Rican president on the spot. It was so successful as a symbol that the United States overreacted to it and interfered directly in Costa Rica's domestic politics.[19]

In 1951 Honduras passed a law establishing a 200-mile claim; then in 1965 the Honduran constitution reverted to a 12-mile territorial sea. Since the 200-mile legislation is still on the books, the actual extent of the Honduran claim is unclear.

El Salvador, in its 1950 constitution, escalated the claims. It claimed the continental shelf, the superjacent waters, and the corresponding air space for a distance of 200 miles over its maritime zone.[20] The claim is repeated in the 1962 constitution.

Other Latin American claims include the 1965 Nicaraguan claim to a 200-mile fishery zone and the 1969 Uruguayan claim to a 200-mile territorial sea. The Uruguayan claim was in the form of a presidential decree, after U.S. diplomatic pressure had blocked legislative passage of a measure claiming only a 200-mile fishery zone.[21]

The most recent Latin American claim was issued by Brazil's President Emílio Médici Garrastazu in March 1970 and called for sovereignty over Brazilian waters 200 miles from shore. The regulations setting forth the Brazilian claim went into effect on June 1, 1971. They provided that the 200-mile claim be divided into two equal parts: in the inner 100-mile zone only Brazilian-flag vessels would be permitted to fish; foreign-flag vessels would be permitted to fish in the outer 100-mile zone if they purchased licenses. Furthermore, no foreign-flag vessels would be allowed to fish for crustaceans anywhere in the 200-mile area.[22]

Another example of a unilaterally claimed extension, although not that of a Latin American nation, was the claim made by Canada in 1970. Despite vigorous protests from the United States, Canada extended her authority 100 miles into the Arctic by setting up a special pollution control zone. The Canadian government was quite united in its concern about the possibility of oil spills and other pollution in the Northwest Passage, especially since technology is on the threshold of achieving year-round transit in the passage. Prime Minister Trudeau admitted that the extension was not supported by international law, but he declared that Canada could not afford to wait until international law caught up with technology.[23]

POTENTIAL HEMISPHERIC CLAIMANTS

Several of the other Latin American nations are known to have similar extensions under consideration. A Colombian legislator, Senator Uribe, has been trying since 1962 to get such a claim adopted by his nation. He argues that Colombia's continental shelf claim lacks precision, that Colombia must be on an equal footing with her neighbors, and that she must conserve her resources, both fish and eroding soil. Despite the suspicions of other Colombian politicians that Senator Uribe is only seeking notoriety, the Colombian Foreign Ministry has discussed a possible offshore extension with Peruvian diplomats.[24]

In 1966 Mexico's legislature added a three-mile fishery zone to the nine-mile territorial sea.[25] This unilateral extension followed a similar extension of the U.S. fishing zone. The Mexican fishing industry wants even greater extensions. The shrimping industry has been concerned for several decades about U.S. shrimping in the Gulf of Mexico; recently significant Cuban shrimping has occurred there as well. On the Pacific coast the Mexican fishing industry is concerned about the necessity for greater protection from the advanced fishing techniques of the maritime nations: U.S. purse seiners, Russian trawlers, and Japanese long-line fishing.[26] Mexico's concerns are multifaceted; not only is it worried about the impact on traditional artisanal coastal fishing and the tourist-oriented sport fishing industry, but the Echeverria government also has embarked on an ambitious program of fisheries development for domestic consumption and export sales.

In 1968 Mexican President Díaz Ordaz declared that the northern half of the Gulf of California, a prime shrimping area, was within Mexican territorial waters. This claim is based on the definition of the gulf's islands as coastal islands--when a boundary is drawn around them as prescribed in the 1951 World Court decision on an Anglo-Norwegian fisheries dispute, the upper part of the gulf is within Mexican territorial waters. In a restrained dissent, the United States protested the unilateral extension in the Gulf of California, as well as the interpretation of the Anglo-Norwegian decision. According to a speech made by President Díaz, the United States was the only nation to protest. Late in 1969 the Mexican Congress approved legislation extending the territorial waters claim from nine to twelve miles--the 1966 extension to twelve miles had set up a fishing zone--and the Mexican government began enforcing the twelve-mile claim in 1970.[27] More recently Mexico has indicated that it supports a 200-mile "patrimonial sea" rather than the territorial sea concept, but it does not intend to make a unilateral claim.

Fishery relations between the United States and Mexico are delicate, for there is extensive shrimping by U.S. vessels in the Gulf of Mexico. There is also considerable fishing by California-based coastal boats licensed to fish within Mexican territorial waters. A new Mexican law governing fishing within Mexico's territorial sea went into effect on January 1, 1973. This law requires at least half of the crews of commercial fishing boats operating in Mexico's waters to be Mexican nationals, who must receive the same pay and benefits as American fishermen doing the same work. This law was based on the conviction that the California boats were exploiting their Mexican crew members by paying them substantially less than their U.S. crew. In 1971, according to Fisheries Minister Hector

Medina Neri, 46 of the 128 licensed California vessels filled out their crews in Ensenada with Mexican crewmen.[28]

U.S. fishermen vigorously protested the law, claiming that it would cause high unemployment among U.S. fishermen. After extended negotiations the Mexican government temporarily agreed to an accord based on an "administrative" interpretation of the new law. This interpretation provides that the 50 percent requirement for Mexican crew members will be applied on a fleet basis rather than by individual boat, that captains and engineers will be exempt, and that vessels with a crew of three or less will be exempt. Since most boats that fish in Mexican waters are either small, family-operated vessels or boats that have traditionally hired Mexican crewmen, this accord satisfies the major fears of the U.S. fishing industry, temporarily at least. The accord also froze the number of U.S. vessels to be licensed at 150 and slightly increased the license .fees which currently provide about $300,000 income annually to the Mexican government. At about the same time this accord was worked out, Mexico began operating ten converted U.S. minesweepers as coastal patrol boats.[29]

There is also potential trouble over fishing rights and territorial boundaries between the United States and the Bahamas. The Bahamas currently has a three-mile territorial limit with a contiguous nine-mile fishing zone. Cuban exiles living in Florida began fishing the rich lobster beds off the Bahamas after they discovered that the Bahamian boundary was not based on a continental shelf claim. Several small boats have been seized and confiscated in an attempt to prevent poaching of valuable resources in an industry that the Bahamas intends, with United Nations help, to develop for its own economy. The Bahamian government believes that in the last seven years American fishermen have taken some $30 million dollars worth of lobsters from Bahamian waters. Prime Minister Lynden Pindling has stated that, with independence attained in 1973, the government will seek approval, at the Law of the Sea Conference, for the "archipelago" principle, which would mean drawing a twelve-mile territorial boundary around all of the 700 islands of the Bahamas.[30]

LATIN AMERICAN CONFERENCES ON TERRITORIAL WATERS

The question of the 200-mile extension is problematical in the Caribbean, where difficulties in overlapping claims could develop. Nevertheless, there is considerable interest in the claims. The Caribbean nations held a conference in Santo Domingo in June 1972 on maritime problems and policies. Despite her concern over potential conflicting claims on offshore oil, Venezuela was particularly concerned that a Caribbean maritime policy be drawn up in advance of the 1974 Law of the Sea Conference, and that it be in accord with the policies of the other Latin American nations. Fifteen nations at the Caribbean conference supported a kind of compromise resolution: territorial seas of twelve miles, with "patrimonial waters" up to a maximum of 200 miles from the coastline. In the "patrimonial waters" the coastal states would hold full sovereignty over the resources of the sea and seabed, but no control over navigation. Jamaica and Guyana abstained because of their commonwealth status; Panama and El Salvador abstained because they already claim 200 miles of territorial waters. Guyana and El Salvador were represented even though they are not truly Caribbean nations, but because they have traditional ties with some of the Caribbean nations.[31]

There have been two earlier conferences on maritime zones held in Latin America--both designed to promote and reinforce territorial claims. In May 1970 nine claiming nations, meeting in Montevideo, adopted the Declaration of Sea Rights upholding the right of all coastal states to "establish the limits of their sovereignty and maritime jurisdiction in accordance with their geographical and geological characteristics." The declaration also affirmed the right of the coastal nations to use the natural resources of the sea and seabed to promote development and raise the standard of living for their citizens.[32]

At Peru's invitation a similar conference was held in Lima in August 1970. Fourteen Latin American and Caribbean nations declared that all countries with seacoasts have the right to claim as much of the sea as necessary to protect both their developed and untapped offshore wealth. The declaration stated that they also have the right to institute controls over and under these areas to prevent contamination by pollution and nuclear weapons. Besides the nine nations already claiming a 200-mile zone, the other signatories were Mexico, Guatemala, Honduras, Costa Rica, and Colombia. Six nations sent representatives but did not sign: landlocked Bolivia and Paraguay; Trinidad and Tobago, Jamaica, and Barbados, because of their nearness to each other and to other neighbors; and Venezuela, because she fears other claims on her offshore petroleum and gas fields. Cuba and Haiti did not attend.[33]

12

THE MEANING OF THE CLAIM

With the number of claimants and the wide variety in language and form of each nation's claim, as well as the differing presidential decrees, legislative acts, and constitutional provisions of the individual claimants, the basic meaning and definition of the claim is vague and open to varying interpretations. It should be pointed out that there is a difference between a 200-mile territorial seas claim and a claim for a 200-mile economic zone. The former would be a claim for complete sovereignty over the 200 miles; the latter is a claim solely to the economic resources within the zone. It is quite clear the Latin American extensions do not uniformly claim full and complete sovereignty. C. Neale Ronning points out that for the 1958 Law of the Sea Conference, the Latin American nations listed limits narrower than 200 miles for their territorial seas claims.[34] The only exception at that time was El Salvador. The others claimed distances of three, six, nine or twelve miles as territorial waters and up to 200 miles as conservation zones, fishery protection zones, "jurisdictional" waters, or similar variations. A noted Latin American authority on international law of the sea also contends that the Latin American claimants are not making claim to wider territorial seas.[35] In addition, David Loring's study of the language of the claims discovered a difference in Latin American jurisprudence between soberanía and the unlimited sovereignty defined in Anglo-Saxon jurisprudence. Soberanía merely means "jurisdiction" and could be limited or qualified in some usages.[36]

For example the claims for soberanía ordinarily have not been considered to restrict navigation or "innocent passage" through the waters or the air space over them. However, a few exceptions have been reported. At least one U.S. military flight between Panama and Chile was forbidden to fly over Peru's 200-mile claim in 1968, and in 1969 the plane carrying Governor Rockefeller's fact-finding mission was under certain restrictions over Ecuadorian and Peruvian waters.[37] The only other publicized interference with "innocent passage" occurred during the heightened tension over boat seizures during 1971. The Ecuadorian naval patrol fired warning shots and halted an unarmed U.S. Navy freighter, the Wyandot. This episode apparently occurred because of the mistaken notion that the Wyandot was the mother ship of a fishery. The upshot of the mistake was that the commander of the Ecuadorian navy was dismissed by President Velasco Ibarra.[38]

13

Although it is clear that the claim could be defined or redefined so as to indicate full sovereignty over offshore waters as a territorial sea, it could also be more clearly defined to restrict the meaning to something less than full sovereignty. The maritime nations could be reassured that full control over navigation and "innocent passage" are not included in the claim. Other delimitations might be acceptable to both sides. Perhaps the claim that would be the clearest would be one defined in terms of a 200-mile economic zone, which would mean jurisdiction over the economic resources in and under the waters. Not only would this be a clarifying distinction, but it is also the compromise most likely to be accepted by the majority of the claimants at the present time.

JUSTIFICATIONS FOR THE CLAIM

Of the number of justifications used to support the extensions, conservation probably has been the most important. It has been pointed out that one authority believes that the 200-mile distance was chosen in order to control the Humboldt Current, since this is believed to be the farthest it ever moves out to sea.[39] This is primarily a biological argument with emphasis on the interdependence of currents and migration of fish.[40] It has also been pointed out that the primary reason for Chile's first 200-mile claim was concern over extensive and destructive whaling practices in the South Pacific. Some 300 foreign whaling vessels were capturing between 15,000 and 20,000 whales every year--the source of 90 percent of the world's whale oil. Latin American whalers were able to capture only about 1 percent of the world's supply of whale oil.[41] Considering the virtual disappearance of certain species of whales, the Chilean concern over conservation was not unrealistic. Another interpretation is that the conservation purpose was twofold: to conserve fisheries as well as guano for Latin American agriculture.[42] The Colombian sponsor of 200-mile legislation wants a Colombian extension in order to protect the fishery resources as well as the rich soil being eroded to sea.[43] The CEP nations officially have claimed that the interrelations between all forms of coastal life and all forms of sea life, biomas or ecosystems, demand conservation for reasons of national self-preservation.

The conservation motive becomes entangled with the nationalistic motive, perhaps almost inextricably. This is particularly true when there are several stocks of fish being sought by several different nations. No species exists in isolation; it has to compete for its food and in turn may become food for another species, which is, in turn, food for still another species in the fishery food chain.[44] Concern about interrelated species is apparent in the anchovy and tuna fisheries off the Peruvian coast.

Economic theory about "common property" resources aids our understanding of the conservation justification. Fish is a "common property" resource. Since there is no sole owner, no one has any economic incentive to protect the resource. This means that no one collects economic rent for the use of the resource. The economic rent, which in other resources is collected by "owners" whose welfare demands conservation, is, in oceanic fisheries, simply divided among all fishermen exploiting the resource. Their competition is for division of the economic rent.[45] Using this theoretical analysis we see that the claiming nations are attempting to exact a fee for the economic rent with their demand for licenses.

Obviously nationalism is a very important component of the justifications. An Ecuadorian foreign minister once said that his nation was merely exercising its rights of "ichthyological patrimony."[46] Several observers have concluded that the main motive was one of nationalism or antiimperialism cloaked in conservation and legalism in order to gain exclusive control over sea resources.[47] In particular this nationalism has taken on antiimperialistic overtones since so many of the newer states, with few prospects of becoming distant-water fishing nations, are extremely sensitive about not losing more of their own resources to the developed nations. They would like to be able to produce more protein for their malnourished people and, perhaps, to find a new export market in fish products. Another aspect of nationalism also is apparent in the claims—that of keeping up with neighboring nations. Particularly where the attitudes toward the neighbors are colored by a traditionally bitter suspicion, offshore extensions have been justified as a means of avoiding a neighbor's comparative advantage in maritime law or domestic chauvinism.

The countries of Latin America's west coast, with extremely narrow continental shelves, presumably have little chance of finding rich offshore petroleum deposits. This geological conformation has been used to justify the 200-mile claim over the offshore waters as a kind of "compensatory justice."[48] It should be noted, however, that recent explorations have discovered high-quality petroleum off the Peruvian coast and a promising natural gas field off Ecuador's coast.[49]

SEIZURES

From 1961 through 1972, 175 U.S. tuna vessels were seized for fishing in disputed waters without licenses. Ecuador seized 125 of them--51 in 1971--and Peru seized 39, and the remaining 11 were seized by other countries (Mexico, Panama, Colombia, and El Salvador).[50] A number of vessels from other nations--primarily Japan, Canada, and Mexico--were also seized. Prior to 1961 there were at least 42 "incidents," including some which could be defined as "seizures," involving U.S. fishing boats and Ecuador or Peru. The records of these incidents are not reliable enough to be included in this tally. The American Tunaboat Association (ATA) which has maintained detailed records of the seizures since 1961, distinguishes between "seizures" and "harassments" or "incidents." A seizure occurs when a fishing boat is forced into port, usually after being forcibly boarded, detained, and, ordinarily, fined. There are several kinds of "incidents," including searches, chases, and firing warning shots at a boat without actually detaining it.

Fines

The total amount of fines and fees paid by boatowners from 1961 through 1972 was $5,070,394.[51] Under the terms of the 1954 Fishermen's Protective Act, the U.S. government reimbursed the boatowners the amount of the fines since it regards the claims as "illegal." Amendments now provide that the boatowners also be reimbursed for other costs associated with the seizures. As the pattern of seizures has continued, the size and punitiveness of the fines, particularly on the part of Ecuador, has increased. The largest single fine to date was the $157,740 fine levied by Ecuador against the largest tuna clipper, the Apollo, at the time of its second seizure in 1971.

Escalation of 1971

During 1971 Ecuador intensified the seizures and escalated the punitiveness of the fines so that there was a

quantum increase in both total seizures and fines over the
preceding years. This increase is explained partly by the
very heavy run of skipjack tuna in 1971 within the Ecuadorian claim. Fishermen were more eager in that year to
catch the smaller skipjack variety rather than the larger,
more valuable yellowfin to avoid a dangerously high mercury
content in the large species. This combination of factors
meant that a larger number of tuna seiners were fishing off
the Ecuadorian coast, which, in turn, meant that the small
Ecuadorian patrol fleet found it easy to catch the unli-
censed vessels. There is some suspicion that the prominence of the nationalistic Ecuadorian navy in the government was also a factor explaining the spate of seizures in
1971.[52] Another explanation interpreted the seizures as
efforts to distract attention from domestic tensions. According to this theory, Velasco ordered the seizures in order to divert the friction between the paratroopers and
the police from possible violence.[53] All these explanations overlook Ecuador's newly acquired leverage in the
dispute because of the oil discovery east of the Andes.
Regardless of the explanation, Ecuador became increasingly
intractable over the dispute. For example, the captain of
the Apollo was warned that his $3 million vessel might be
confiscated outright if it were caught again within the
Ecuadorian claim area without a license.

Efforts to Resist Seizures

The sum of seizures and fines does not illuminate the
full magnitude of the problems caused by the seizures.
Numerous other vessels, primarily of U.S. ownership, have
been harassed or fired upon. Approximately 25 of the
seizures have involved gunfire causing some property damage, one serious injury, and considerable risk of explo-
sion, sinking, and death. Since fishing boats are traditionally unprotected militarily, U.S. tuna clippers rely
on their bravado and skill to protect them against seizure.
If their nets are set, however, they are unable to move.
Some have been able to outrun or outmaneuver the patrol
vessels, or to disappear into fog or darkness. In 1963,
when two boats were seized 13 miles off the Ecuadorian
coast, they were joined in port by 19 other U.S. boats
protesting the seizures. Fines of $26,272 were paid and
the other vessels were not held or charged. This episode
intensified U.S. efforts to arrange a modus vivendi on the
dispute. In a more recent Peruvian seizure on February 14,

1969, after one U.S. tuna boat had been forced into port, another, the San Juan, defied surrender orders. She was subsequently chased for two hours and raked with more than 60 rounds of machine-gun fire. Eventually six sister vessels of the San Juan formed a line and bore down on the Peruvian gunboat in an attempt to ram it. At that point the patrol boat halted its attack. No one was injured aboard the San Juan, but she suffered an estimated $50,000 in damages.[54]

Seizure Ritual

The fact that there have not been more serious results from the seizures can be attributed to the orders of the boatowners to cooperate when hailed by a patrol boat, which means that the seizure ritual has become somewhat stylized. The ATA requests radio notification of the time and place of the seizure, if possible, so that it can request U.S. officials to meet the vessel at the nearest port and arrange for its release. In fact the ATA credits the Fishermen's Protective Act with prevention of bloodshed. Since the U.S. fishermen know that they will be released and eventually reimbursed, they are willing to cooperate with the patrol boats and other officials. They are very concerned, however, that the same kind of restraint might not always characterize the behavior of the patrol boat personnel--they especially fear impetuous or intoxicated patrol boat captains. Despite the ritual of seizures, there is an ever-present chance of heated tempers exploding into a less stylized situation.[55]

U.S. Military Assistance and Latin American Patrol Boats

One feature of the seizures which is particularly rankling to the U.S. tuna fishermen is the fact that several of the Ecuadorian and Peruvian patrol boats are obsolescent U.S. vessels that were given, sold, or loaned to the Latin American navies or governments under provisions of U.S. military assistance. Nine of the Ecuadorian navy's 21 vessels have been provided as part of U.S. military assistance. Under terms of a naval lease program, a variety of support vessels were leased to the Ecuadorian navy: a net-laying boat, a drydock, an ocean tug, a floating workshop, a water barge, and a transport vessel.

There is also a government loan program that gave the Ecuadorian government two patrol boats from November 1960 to November 1965. These vessels are known to have participated in a number of seizures--the tuna industry alleges that they were involved in 21 of the first 25 seizures of 1971. Also it has been pointed out that no vessels that have been "loaned" to any government have ever been returned.[56] Although the tuna industry has urged cancellation of the ship loan program and the enforced return of the loaned vessels, it should be clear that such action would not stop the seizures. As a matter of fact both the Peruvian and Ecuadorian navies have acquired new patrol vessels from Europe. The effectiveness of their patrols does not hinge on the acquisition of obsolescent vessels from the United States. In its frustrations over the seizures, the tuna industry found more evidence of the Pentagon's alleged perfidy in a goodwill visit of the U.S. submarine Blackfin to the Ecuadorian navy in Guayaquil in November 1971, a month during which Ecuador seized 20 U.S. fishing boats.[57] The visit could have been an accident of timing, although it also could have been an attempt to reassure Ecuador.

Rate of Seizures

The rate of seizures reflects both fishing and political developments. Peru seized six U.S. vessels in 1955 and seven in 1967 but made only three seizures in the intervening years. The increase in her seizures since the mid-1960s reflects Peru's new prominence as a fishing nation as well as the powerful influence of nationalism in Peruvian politics. Between 1951 and 1956 Ecuador seized 13 U.S. boats. In 1963 she seized only two vessels, but her actions caused 19 other vessels to protest. Following both intensified U.S. diplomatic pressures,[58] as well as chaotic changes in Ecuador's government, a military junta assumed power. The United States negotiated a secret agreement with the junta, agreeing to recognize a 12-mile limit instead of the still "official" three-mile limit if Ecuador would relinquish the other 188 miles. This agreement successfully prevented seizures until public knowledge of it toppled the junta. The succeeding government naturally renounced the agreement.[59] Since then the junta has been excoriated, the 200-mile claim to territorial seas has been reasserted with a vengeance, and the rate of Ecuadorian seizures has risen sharply. Furthermore the new government tripled the licensing fee from $12 to $35 per net registered ton per vessel.[60]

Seizure Profits

One other fact illuminating Ecuadorian seizures is that the Ecuadorian navy has a direct financial stake in them. A 1969 Ecuadorian law gives the navy 70 percent of the total collected in fines.[61] Not only does a seizure accord nationalistic prestige to the navy, it puts a cash premium on seizing large vessels as well. Under the terms of this law, the Ecuadorian navy collected a bounty worth nearly $1,750,000 in 1971.

DIPLOMACY AND THE 200-MILE CLAIM

There have been a number of attempts to settle the claims dispute by negotiation since it began two decades ago. These attempts have been made through international organizations, using direct negotiations with the CEP claimants as a body and bilateral negotiations between the United States and one of the claimants. The State Department has made repeated and patient efforts to reach an acceptable solution, either in terms of international law or in terms of a working agreement. In particular the Office of Special Assistant to the Secretary of State for Fisheries and Wildlife, now held by Donald L. McKernan, and previously held by Wilbert McLeod Chapman and William Herrington, has worked diligently to settle the issue and to reassure Congress that a settlement is possible. Their efforts have been persistent and imaginative, but fruitless; they yielded limited success at best, and some attempts merely stiffened the claimants' resistance to compromise. In general, failure to settle the issue is attributable to the lack of compelling reasons to do so on the part of the Latin American claimants.

Santiago Conference

After the CEP powers turned down the first U.S. proposal to let the World Court arbitrate, the United States proposed a four-power conference to discuss fishery conservation rather than the legitimacy of the claims. The conference was held in Santiago in 1955 but it accomplished

20

little because the positions were already stalemated with the underdeveloped coastal nations versus the developed maritime nation. The CEP nations viewed the issue as one of foreign plunder of their valuable natural resources without compensation: distant-water fishing was the newest example of exploitative foreign capitalism or imperialism.

The U.S. delegation proposed establishing an international conservation commission to regulate fishing vessels, with each member to have one vote and each nation to enforce compliance by its own fishing boats. The CEP nations rejected this, demanding instead a 12-mile limit plus "areas traditionally exploited." This was unacceptable to the United States because it would have allowed each coastal state to claim 200 miles as "traditional."

The most extraordinary feature of the Santiago negotiations was the unique CEP ecological theory to give scientific justification for their claimed extension. According to the theory, "ecosystems," or "biomas," are interdependencies linking all varieties of coastal life with all varieties of sea life. The U.S. delegation responded that the meteorological and oceanographic conditions determining the richness of the coastal waters originate much farther away than 200 miles and cannot be related to national boundaries.[62] In the beginning many international legal experts regarded the "ecosystem" justification with astonishment. Today there is greater appreciation for the legitimacy of the ecological rationale, even though no 200-mile claim can guarantee the conservation of migratory fish.

Inter-American Diplomacy

Attempts to settle the dispute also were made through inter-American channels. These efforts worked to the diplomatic disadvantage of the United States. Rather than achieving a hemispheric agreement limiting the unilateral expansion of claims, they enabled the CEP powers to reap significant hemispheric support for the principles of expansion. No doubt this increased support was partially an exercise in Yankee-baiting, but it also signaled anew the increasing friction between the coastal and maritime nations.

The Hispanic-Luso-American Congress of International Law, in its 1953 meeting in São Paulo, passed a resolution supporting the right of coastal nations to supervise fishing and whaling over the continental shelf or within waters

200 miles from shore. The Inter-American Council of Jurists, an official committee of international lawyers of the OAS members, began as early as 1950 to study the issue of territorial seas. A draft convention prepared by the Inter-American Juridical Commission also took the position that a coastal state had the right to sovereignty over the continental shelf and the waters above it, as well as the right to protect the resources in the sea up to 200 miles offshore. The Tenth Inter-American Conference, meeting in Caracas in 1954, passed a resolution supportive of the continental shelf claims. Another meeting of the Inter-American Council of Jurists, held in Mexico City in 1956, made a preparatory study for the OAS Conference on the Continental Shelf and Conservation held later that year at Ciudad Trujillo. With a vote of 15 to 1 (5 abstentions), the delegates resolved that each state was competent to establish its own territorial waters within "reasonable limits" by taking into account geographical, geological, biological, economic, and security factors.[63] When the Ciudad Trujillo conference convened, it accepted a U.S. proposal that no final decisions be made except by unanimous vote, which meant that it could make no final decisions on the width of territorial seas. Ultimately, the Ciudad Trujillo conference merely listed the points of agreement and disagreement in order to clarify the situation for possible future settlement. This impasse ended OAS efforts to deal with the issue until 1971.

U.N. Conferences on the Law of the Sea

The next attempts at settlement were held under U.N. auspices in two conferences on the law of the sea held in 1958 and 1960. The situation was much the same--the scene was changed and there were additional players, but the dialogue was repetitive of earlier diplomatic efforts. The growing number of newly independent, developing coastal nations repudiated the "exploitation" of offshore resources by developing maritime powers. In addition rapid advances in technology heightened the rivalries to control undersea resources.[64] Some authorities suspect, in fact, that the coastal nations are less concerned about resource conservation than they are about their exclusive exploitation of "their" resources.[65] The landlocked nations have resisted such exclusive control with vigor.[66]

In both U.N. conferences the United States worked for a compromise acceptable to both coastal and maritime nations,

which meant getting concessions from those nations opposed
to ending the three-mile limit, as well as reducing the
Latin American claims. In 1960 the United States and Canada jointly proposed a six-mile territorial sea with an
additional six-mile fishing zone. This proposal was
amended--in an effort to secure Latin American support--
to provide that a coastal nation could extend its fishing
zone farther if there were scientific justifications,
which were to be determined at a hearing of coastal and
maritime nations. The amended proposal was defeated by
one vote--the U.N. barely missed achieving a compromise on
territorial waters limitations. Ecuador had tentatively
agreed to abstain if the United States would immediately
recognize a 12-mile territorial sea off her coast. Later
Ecuador also insisted that the United States withdraw its
amended claim and those claims of U.S. nationals for reimbursement of fines and damages. Since the U.S. delegation
had no authority to relinquish private claims, it was unable to meet Ecuador's terms for abstention. Chile apparently had intended to support the amended resolution, but
Peru exacted Chile's pledge to the Declaration of Santiago.
The three CEP countries, as well as Venezuela, Mexico, and
Panama, were among the 28 nations that opposed the compromise "six-plus-six" zone.[67] It should be noted that the
primary efforts of the U.S. delegation were to break the
unanimity of the CEP nations rather than to persuade another opposition vote to abstain or to vote affirmatively.
Delegates from the nations claiming 200 miles felt that
they were treated high-handedly since they were singled
out as being "on trial" because of their claims.[68] Realis-
tically, however, it is obvious that even had the compromise reached the two-thirds vote required, without agreement by the Latin American claimants to relinquish their
claims, the compromise would not have had much meaning in
"Latin American waters." Nor, it should be added, was it
assured that a nation's position in conference would be
the same one proclaimed in legislation or decree.

Since the 1960 conference a number of nations have
adopted a 12-mile territorial sea or fishing zone. The
coastal fishermen pressured the United States to do so,
and in 1966 unilateral legislation was enacted establishing a 12-mile U.S. fishing zone.[69]

Since 1969 the United Nations has reopened discussions of the 1958 Convention on the Continental Shelf in
an effort to revise the definition of the shelf. The
original convention defined the continental shelf as extending to the 200-meter depth or to that depth which is

23

"exploitable." The exploitability definition means that
the only limitation on national claims to continental
shelves is technology--and that is advancing rapidly in
the developed nations. The U.N. Committee on Uses of the
Sea-bed and Ocean Floor Beyond National Jurisdiction has
been meeting since 1970 in preparation for the next Law of
the Sea Conference, now scheduled for June-August 1974.

Bilateral Diplomatic Efforts

The State Department has made repeated efforts to
achieve bilateral agreement with the individual claimants.
Since the 200-mile claim has become a point of national
honor, however, the State Department has recognized that
it is unrealistic to expect either Ecuador or Peru to relinquish their claims officially. Therefore the department's diplomatic efforts have sought a practical arrangement on conservation and seizures, leaving the 200-mile
claim intact as far as the claimants are concerned, but
unrecognized as far as the United States is concerned.
There have been three informal treaties, or modi vivendi,
with the CEP nations, in addition to one near miss.

In 1955, after the four-power Santiago conference
stalemated, representatives of the U.S. tuna industry were
invited to Lima, where a kind of face-saving working agreement was worked out. There had been a long tradition of
bait boats purchasing licenses in order to fish for bait
within the three-mile limit. This practice had begun after World War I and was common for U.S. boats fishing off
Mexico or the Galápagos Islands. Accordingly, the current
ATA president, Dr. Wilbert M. Chapman, persuaded the Peruvian government to phrase the license in such a way that
U.S. fishermen could buy licenses without implying acceptance of the legitimacy of the offshore claim. Thus the
licenses merely said that they gave the purchaser the
right to fish within Peruvian waters, without any mention
of what the boundaries were. This meant that U.S. bait
boats could purchase licenses under the guise of acquiring
bait in a traditionally acceptable manner, but were not
subject to seizure anywhere within the 200 miles.[70] Peru's
President Manuel Odría issued a decree on January 5, 1956--
"Regulations Governing the Issuance of Fishing Permits to
Foreign Vessels in the Jurisdictional Waters of Peru"--
which spelled out the details of the agreement. It also
provided that funds acquired by the sale of licenses were
to be allocated for maritime research.[71]

During the same year Secretary of State Dulles report-edly got a tentative agreement in principle from Peru's President Manuel Prado Ugarteche on the occasion of the latter's inauguration. The secret agreement provided that Peru would drop its 200-mile claim in return for a conser-vation plan for the South Pacific modeled after the North Pacific fisheries agreement. This meant that the fishing fleets of signatory countries would have had the right to fish in the South Pacific if they observed conservation measures. On his return trip to Washington Dulles appar-ently was favorably received in Quito, where he spent one day discussing such an agreement with Ecuadorian officials. A premature report of these negotiations published by the New York Times caused chagrin in Lima and surprise in Quito and Santiago. Prado hastened to reassure Peru's CEP partners that Peru would remain faithful to the Declara-tion of Santiago and would not abrogate the claim either in secret negotiations or in practice.[72]

In December 1957, 23 U.S. fishing boats became in-volved in a dispute with Chile which was settled by an in-formal agreement similar to that with Peru. The U.S. fishing boats refused to halt when signal shots were fired. Later the Chilean navy ordered the fishing boats into port for inspection and payment of a $1,200 fine per boat, but the boats sailed toward Peruvian waters. The dispute was settled by an agreement reached between representatives of the ATA and Chile. Under its terms the fines against the 23 boats were canceled and ATA boats agreed to buy licenses at $100 each for six-month periods plus a payment of $12 per net registered ton per vessel for 100 days.[73]

A technological innovation--the introduction of nylon nets--made the bait boats obsolescent. Use of nylon nets led to purse seining for tuna, eliminating the need for bait and thereby removing the necessity for catching bait within the three-mile limit. This in turn eliminated the subterfuge behind the ATA-Peruvian accord and the ATA-Chilean accord; the tuna vessels stopped buying licenses and the Peruvian seizures began again.[74]

A more official modus vivendi was negotiated between the United States and Ecuador. During the 1963-66 period, when a military junta governed Ecuador, a secret treaty was negotiated in which the United States agreed to recog-nize a 12-mile territorial sea for Ecuador in return for Ecuador's relinquishing the other 188 miles. When details of the agreement were published by the Quito newspaper El Tiempo, on June 18, 1965, the junta was stigmatized; the government of Provisional President Clemente Yerovi Indaburu,

25

which replaced the junta in 1966, repudiated the treaty. Since then the 200-mile claim to a territorial sea has been affirmed as national dogma in Ecuador's constitution and the rate of seizures and fines has increased dramatically.[75]

Quadripartite Fisheries Conference

In 1969 and 1970 there were intermittent talks between the United States and the CEP nations--the Quadripartite Fisheries Conference--on ways to achieve a practical compromise solution of the dispute. The CEP representatives rejected U.S. proposals for international licensing agencies that would license all boats in the disputed waters. They demanded that the United States eliminate the 35 percent ad valorem tariff on fish canned in oil, as well as labeling restrictions that prevent bonito from being marketed in the United States as tuna.[76] There was also some impression that the United States might be willing to offer economic assistance if seizures ceased in regulated conservation zones.[77] There was considerable hope in 1970 that these talks might lead closer to settlement of the dispute, especially since each side was effecting leverage on the other side. A legislative proposal pending at that time before the U.S. Congress would have provided economic sanctions against all fishery products imported from any nation that seized U.S. fishing boats. Passage of this legislation would have been quite damaging to Peru's important fishmeal industry. Since 1971, however, Ecuador has refused to participate in the negotiations and the hopes of such a conference reaching a satisfactory settlement have diminished.

Special 1971 Session of the OAS

The events of 1971 heightened and escalated the diplomatic drama. The outrage of the tuna industry over the first 11 Ecuadorian seizures in 1971 brought about a ban on arms sales to Ecuador for one year. Secretary of State William P. Rogers acted under the terms of the Foreign Military Sales Act, which provides that arms sales, credits, and guarantees can be suspended for one year after a nation seizes a U.S. fishing boat in "international" waters. Rogers also informed the Ecuadorian ambassador that the remainder of the planned $29 million in U.S. foreign aid to Ecuador for 1971 was being placed under review.[78]

At the time of the sanction the Council of the OAS was meeting in Washington, discussing ways to combat hemispheric terrorism. Ecuador took admirable advantage of the timing by turning the issue of sanctions into an arena that would naturally pit the OAS member nations against the United States. This skillful maneuver came when Ecuador charged that the United States had violated Article 19 of the OAS charter and asked for an emergency council session to deal with the charge. Article 19 states: "No state may use or encourage the use of coercive measures of an economic or political character in order to force the sovereign will of another state and obtain from it advantages of any kind." In an attempt to forestall such a special session, the United States first proposed referring the dispute to the five-nation Inter-American Committee on Peaceful Settlement (Colombia, Costa Rica, Paraguay, Dominican Republic, and the United States), and then proposed submitting the dispute to the World Court for a "binding" decision or reopening the quadripartite negotiations, which were due to reconvene later in 1971. The OAS voted 22 to 0, however, with the United States abstaining, to convoke the special session to hear Ecuador's charges that the United States had violated Article 19.

Ultimately the special session adopted a mild, vaguely worded resolution calling on the United States and Ecuador to resume talks on their differences and to settle through negotiations. The resolution, adopted by a vote of 19 to 0 (4 abstentions), urged Ecuador and the United States to "avoid an aggravation of their differences" and to "refrain from utilizing any measures which affect the sovereignty of the states and the tranquillity of the hemisphere."[79] A three-nation negotiating team--Mexico, Argentina, and Guatemala--worked out a resolution recommending "early" resumption of the four-power fisheries talks.[80] Within a few days Ecuador expelled the U.S. military mission, consisting of about 30 members. Since then Ecuador has refused to negotiate in the Quadripartite Fisheries Conference and has refused terms offered privately by U.S. diplomats as long as the arms-sales ban remains in effect.

U.N. Law of the Sea Conference, 1974

The U.S. officials, in their frustration with other efforts, have banked increasingly on the U.N. Law of the Sea Conference, hoping that it will be able to achieve a universally accepted international treaty governing uses

27

of the oceans. Originally this conference was tentatively scheduled for 1972, but it has been postponed several times. It was scheduled for June 1974 in Caracas.

The planning for this conference has been intricate and time-consuming. The problems are more than technical; they are political. For example when the United States introduced the only complete draft proposal on seabeds to the U.N. Seabeds Committee in 1970, the other nations, whose positions had not been completely thought out, were suspicious.[81] The approcah of the State Department to the problems of the multiple uses of the oceans typically has favored compromises within a technical administrative framework, with an international regime making decisions on "apolitical" grounds. The coastal nations do not make the same assumption; they know that the rules, voting powers, and procedures approved for an international regime will be established by political decisions, and that the political decisions will color all the technical ones that follow. These nations, with the support of the Soviet Union and China, oppose an international regime controlling the seabed and fisheries as a continuation of capitalist control and sophisticated neocolonialism.[82]

In preparing for the Law of the Sea Conference the United States has proposed a draft convention covering several articles, which deal with the seabeds, the breadth of territorial seas, international straits, and an international sea tribunal to provide for settlement of disputes over uses of the oceans and fisheries. In general terms the draft convention proposes that the territorial seas be limited to 12 nautical miles with a provision for freedom of navigation and overflight through international straits. President Nixon proposed the renunciation of national claims to seabed resources beyond a depth of 200 meters, with the exploitation of the rest of the seabed resources to be controlled internationally.[83]

The U.S. draft fisheries article was submitted to the U.N. Seabeds Committee in 1972.[84] Its major theme is that the biological nature of each species, rather than arbitrary national boundary lines, should determine the nature of the conservation and fishing controls. For coastal species and anadromous (those which go upriver to spawn) species, the coastal state shall regulate and have preferential fishing rights beyond their territorial seas throughout the entire migratory range of the species. The coastal state can reserve to its vessels that portion of such resources that they can harvest annually. As the coastal state's fishing capacity expands, so shall its preferential fishing right.

28

For highly migratory oceanic species, including tuna, the draft proposes that they be regulated by international fishery organizations, to which any nation whose vessels harvest or intend to harvest the species would have an equal right of participation. The regulations of this organization would apply to all vessels regardless of their national registry. Both in coastal species and in highly migratory species the principles of maximum sustainable yield would be used to determine the allowable catch.

The draft recommends that coastal states may reserve to their flag vessels the portion of the allowable annual catch that they can harvest. All other states, without discrimination, including those whose vessels have traditionally fished for a resource and those which are land-locked or which have had limited access to a resource, would be allowed access to that portion of the resource not reserved for the vessels of the coastal state. If necessary, to accommodate the allocations to the coastal nations, traditional fishing may be reduced and all nations fishing for a resource may be required to pay reasonable fees to share the cost of regulating the fishing.

Regarding enforcement the U.S. draft proposes that a coastal state may inspect and arrest vessels for violations of its regulations. It may try and punish these vessels unless a vessel's nation of registry provides for trial and punishment for violation of another nation's coastal fishing regulations. In this case the home nation would try the violator within six months. In the case of violations of the regulations of international fishery organizations, each state shall make it an offense for its vessels to violate the regulations. Authorized officials may inspect for violations but the flag state of the violator shall have the jurisdiction for trial and punishment, also to be disposed of within six months. Any disputes between states shall be submitted to a special commission of five members unless the disputants find another way to resolve the issue.

The complexities of the draft convention illustrate the problems of formulating U.S. foreign policy on maritime law. The State Department must attempt to devise policy that will accommodate a wide variety of species as well as juggle the seemingly contradictory domestic interests--the distant-water fisheries, the coastal fisheries, the navy, the petroleum industry; and international interests--less developed coastal nations, maritime states with traditional fishing fleets, and even landlocked and other underdeveloped nations. The U.S. draft convention is a comprehensive plan offering something for everybody,

yet not completely satisfactory to any one nation or interest. The one element completely missing from the draft,
however, is any version of a 200-mile claim. The United
States remains opposed to unilateral extensions for any
purpose because they fail to accommodate the international
nature of the problems. It is opposed to the 200-mile de-
limitation for the same reason.

It seems unlikely that the claimants will reduce their
claims in terms of distance. They get considerable mileage
domestically and internationally from the claims as pioneers
in maritime law. Several Asian and African nations, including Ghana, Guinea, South Korea, Pakistan, India, Ceylon, and
Sierra Leone, have made claims for extensions, usually for
fishery protection zones. In view of this trend the Latin
American claimants believe that international law of the
sea is evolving, under their leadership, toward extension
of specialized zones for fisheries, conservation, and pollution control. Therefore it is not likely that they will
relinquish the 200-mile terminology.

It is far more likely that they will be willing to re-
define their claims in terms of less than complete sovereignty over the 200 miles. The proposal apparently winning
the most support is similar to the distinction made at the
Caribbean conference on maritime problems between a 12-mile
territorial sea and a 200-mile "patrimonial sea." At one
time Peru's delegate to the U.N. Seabeds Committee even
suggested that Peru might relinquish its claim for complete
sovereignty while retaining the claim for the natural resources in and under its waters.[85] When the Inter-American
Juridical Commission of the OAS met in Rio de Janeiro in
February 1973, the Peruvian delegates, supported by Brazil
and Colombia, opposed the division of the waters into two
zones--territorial seas and patrimonial seas. The other
delegates, excepting the abstentions of Argentina and
Trinidad and Tobago, supported this distinction.[86]

Venezuela, Mexico, and Colombia introduced a joint
draft convention for the treaty on law of the sea to the
U.N. General Assembly on April 2, 1973.[87] This draft proposal embodies the patrimonial sea concept, with the coastal state having the sovereign right to the natural resources in the waters, the seabed, and the subsoil. According to the proposal, the coastal state has the right
to adopt measures necessary to insure its sovereignty and
to prevent pollution; the coastal state shall regulate research, exploration, and exploitation of renewable and
nonrenewable resources in the patrimonial sea; and the
patrimonial sea cannot exceed a distance of 200 miles

from shore. It also stipulates that other states have the right of free navigation and overflights in the patrimonial sea, and that the coastal state shall respect the freedom to lay submarine cables and pipelines.

It should be noted that Venezuela has become the chief spokesman for the patrimonial sea proposal. It also appears that she has enough supporters to isolate the Peruvian position as that of a diehard on territoriality. If the maritime nations, especially the United States, accept this sort of compromise, the treaty on the law of the sea will probably be negotiated. There are some indications that this acceptance is possible. For example, in recent negotiations between Ecuador and the United States, State Department officials have offered to submit a proposal to Congress authorizing governmental purchase of fishing licenses in return for navigational access beyond a 12-mile limit. It is not clear what congressional reaction would be--conceivably enough members could be persuaded by the economy of license purchases compared to reimbursement of seizures. The Pentagon is clearly and adamantly opposed to license purchase or fishery agreements, which imply a de facto acceptance of the 200-mile terminology.[88] It is equally clear that the Latin American claimants are not likely to accept any treaty which does not incorporate a 200-mile economic zone.

NOTES

1. Thomas Wolff, "Peruvian-United States Relations Over Maritime Fishing, 1945-1969," Occasional Paper No. 4 (Kingston, R.I.: The Law of the Sea Institute, March 1970), p. 2.

2. Marjorie M. Whiteman, Digest of International Law, vol. 4 (Washington: Government Printing Office, 1965), pp. 945-62.

3. Presidential Proclamation No. 2667, September 28, 1945.

4. Teodoro Alvarado Garaicoa, "The Continental Shelf and the Extension of Territorial Waters," Miami Law Quarterly 10, no. 4 (Summer 1956): 493.

5. Argentina's Law on Sovereignty over Seas and Seabed Off Its Coast, Law 17.094, December 29, 1966, International Legal Materials 6 (1967): 663-64.

6. Sergio Teitelboim, "Los paises del Pacifico Sur y el mar territorial," Estudios Internacionales 4, no. 13 (April-June 1970): 40.

7. Latin America 6, no. 52 (December 29, 1972).

8. John A. Knauss, "Factors Influencing a U.S. Position in a Future Law of the Sea Conference," Occasional Paper No. 10 (Kingston, R.I.: The Law of the Sea Institute, April 1971), p. 14.

9. Andres A. Aramburu y Menchaca, "Character and Scope of the Rights Declared and Practiced over the Continental Sea and Shelf," American Journal of International Law 47, no. 1 (January 1953): 120-23.

10. David C. Loring, "The United States-Peruvian 'Fisheries' Dispute," Stanford Law Review 23, no. 3 (February 1971): 400.

11. Presidential Declaration (Chile), June 23, 1947; Supreme Decree No. 781 (Peru), August 1, 1947; Laws and Regulations on the Regime of the High Seas, I (New York: United Nations Legislative Series, 1951) ST/Leg/SER.B/1, pp. 6-8, 16-18.

12. Whiteman, op. cit., pp. 1092-96. See also Henry Reiff, The United States and the Treaty Law of the Sea (Minneapolis: University of Minnesota Press, 1959), pp. 306-07; and Josef L. Kunz, "Continental Shelf and International Law: Confusion and Abuse," American Journal of International Law 50, no. 4 (October 1960): 764.

13. Whiteman, op. cit., pp. 1062-70.

14. James C. Carey, Peru and the United States, 1900-1962 (Notre Dame, Ind.: University of Notre Dame Press, 1964), p. 197.

15. Rudolph Gomez, The Peruvian Administrative System (Boulder: University of Colorado Press, 1969), p. 23.

16. George Maier, "The Boundary Dispute Between Ecuador and Peru," American Journal of International Law 63, no. 1 (January 1969): 42-46; Mary Jeanne Reid Martz, "Ecuador and the Eleventh Inter-American Conference," Journal of Inter-American Studies 10, no. 2 (April 1968). See also George Maier, The Ecuadorian Presidential Election of June 2, 1968: An Analysis (Washington: Institute for the Comparative Study of Political Systems, 1969), pp. 21-25; and David H. Zook, Jr., Zarumilla-Marañon: Ecuador-Peru Dispute (New York: Bookman Associates, 1964), pp. 223-29.

17. Dale Vernon Slaght, "The Ecuadorian Image of Peru: A Study of Changing Elite Perceptions," unpublished Ph.D. dissertation, American University, 1972.

18. New York Times, January 28, 1967, p. 54.

19. Loring, op. cit., p. 437.

20. F. V. Garcia Amador, The Exploitation and Conservation of the Resources of the Sea: A Study of Con-

temporary International Law, 2d ed. (Leyden: A. W. Sythoff, 1963), pp. 99-100.

21. Uruguay, Decree 235, May 16, 1969, Extending Territorial Waters; Loring, op. cit., p. 437.

22. Brazil: Decree-Law Extending Territorial Sea to 200 Miles, March 25, 1970, International Legal Materials 10 (1971): 1224-33. See also Los Angeles Times, June 2, 1971, p. 17 and June 10, 1971, p. 1.

23. Arctic Waters Pollution Prevention Act, c. 47 (Canada, 1970), Royal Assent Given June 26, 1970. Reprinted in International Legal Materials 9 (1970): 543. See also New York Times, April 19, 1970, p. 9 and April 26, 1970, p. 3.

24. Los Angeles Times, May 13, 1969, p. 13.

25. David W. Windley, "International Practice Regarding Traditional Fishing Privileges of Foreign Fishermen in Zones of Extended Maritime Jurisdiction," American Journal of International Law 63, no. 3 (July, 1969), 496.

26. Los Angeles Times, September 2, 1969, p. 1.

27. Los Angeles Times, January 4, 1970, p. 5.

28. Los Angeles Times, June 16, 1972, p. 6.

29. Los Angeles Times, February 4, 1972, p. 12.

30. Christian Science Monitor, January 26, 1973, p. 4.

31. Specialized Conference of Caribbean Countries Concerning the Problems of the Sea: Declaration of Santo Domingo, June 9, 1972. Reprinted in International Legal Materials 11, no. 4 (July 1972): 892-93. See also Latin America 6, no. 19 (May 12, 1972) and 6, no. 24 (June 16, 1972).

32. Declaration of Montevideo on the Law of the Sea, May 8, 1970, Nine-Nation Territorial Limits Conference, Montevideo, Uruguay. See also New York Times, May 10, 1970, p. 14.

33. Latin American Meeting on Aspects of the Law of the Sea: Declaration and Resolutions, Lima, August 4-8, 1970. Reprinted in International Legal Materials 10 (1971): 207-14. See also New York Times, August 16, 1970, p. 21.

34. C. Neale Ronning, Law and Politics in Inter-American Diplomacy (New York: John Wiley & Sons, 1963), pp. 110-11.

35. Garcia Amador, op. cit., pp. 76-79.

36. Loring, op. cit., pp. 399, 401.

37. Los Angeles Times, August 17, 1969, p. 2.

38. Los Angeles Times, March 13, 1971, p. 8, March 14, 1971, p. 2.

39. Aramburu y Menchaca, op. cit., pp. 120-23.

40. S. A. Bayitch, Inter-American Law of Fisheries (New York: Oceana Publications, 1957), p. 14.

41. Kunz, op. cit., pp. 849-50.

42. Barry B. L. Auguste, The Continental Shelf: Practice and Policy of the Latin American States with Special Reference to Chile, Ecuador and Peru (Geneva: Librarie E. Droz, 1960), pp. 165-84.

43. Los Angeles Times, May 13, 1969, p. 13.

44. Food and Agriculture Organization, The State of the World's Fisheries (Rome: FAO, 1968), p. 16.

45. James Crutchfield and Arnold Zellner, Economic Aspects of the Pacific Halibut Fishery, Fishery Industrial Research 1, no. 1 (Washington: Department of the Interior, 1963), pp. 15-20; James Crutchfield, "The Marine Fisheries: A Problem in International Cooperation," American Economic Review 54, no. 3 (May 1964): 207-18.

46. New York Times, March 12, 1967, sec. 4.

47. Shigeru Oda, International Control of Sea Resources (Leyden: A. W. Sythoff, 1963), p. 18; Francis T. Christy, Jr. and Anthony Scott, The Common Wealth in Ocean Fisheries: Some Problems of Growth and Economic Allocation (Baltimore: Johns Hopkins Press, 1965), p. 183; Crutchfield, op. cit., p. 214.

48. Juraj Andrassy, International Law and the Resources of the Sea (New York: Columbia University Press, 1970), p. 44; Myres S. McDougal and William T. Burke, The Public Order of the Oceans: A Contemporary International Law of the Sea (New Haven: Yale University Press, 1962), pp. 74-75.

49. Wall Street Journal, September 22, 1971, p. 9 and March 2, 1970, p. 8.

50. American Tunaboat Association Newsletter, January 19, 1973.

51. Ibid.

52. Latin America 5, no. 23 (June 9, 1972).

53. Wall Street Journal, February 17, 1972, p. 1.

54. The American Fishery and Cannery Worker 6, no. 2 (February 1969): 104. See also Los Angeles Times, February 15, 1969, p. 1 and February 16, 1969, sec. A.

55. Interview conducted by the authors with August Fellando, general manager of the American Tunaboat Association, San Diego, California, September 6, 1972.

56. Congressional Record 117, no. 189 (December 6, 1971), H 11819-27.

57. New York Times, November 29, 1971.

58. "Ecuador-United States Fisheries Dispute: Statement of the Secretary of State," Department of State,

Press Release no. 303 (June 5, 1963); International Legal Materials 2 (1963): 812.

59. New York Times, April 14, 1968, sec. 4. See also Loring, op. cit., p. 408.

60. Instituto Nacional de Pesca, "Estadisticas de la actividad pesquera en el Ecuador," Boletin Informativo 3, no. 2 (September 1968): 39-41.

61. Registro Oficial, Numero 132, March 10, 1969, No. 110-CL, Ley de Pesca y Fomento Pesquero, Tit. IX, Art. 71.

62. U.S. Department of State, Santiago Negotiations on Fishery Conservation Problems (Washington: Government Printing Office, 1955), pp. 1-11.

63. Oda, op. cit., pp. 38-39.

64. Teodoro Alvarado Garaicoa, El dominio del mar (Guayaquil: Departamento de Publicaciones de la Universidad de Guayaquil, Ecuador, 1968), pp. 149-95; Daniel S. Cheever, "The Role of International Organization in Ocean Development," International Organization 22, no. 3 (Summer 1968): 629-48. For a thorough study of the leadership role taken by one less-developed nation see Morris Davis, Iceland Extends Its Fisheries Limits (Stockholm: Scandinavian University Books, 1963), chap. 5.

65. Douglas M. Johnston, The International Law of Fisheries: A Framework for Policy-Oriented Inquiries (New Haven: Yale University Press, 1965), pp. 321-57.

66. Martin Ira Glasser, Access to the Sea for Developing Landlocked States (The Hague: Martinus Nijhoff, 1970).

67. Arthur H. Dean, "The Second Geneva Conference on the Law of the Sea: The Fight for Freedom of the Seas," American Journal of International Law 54, no. 4 (October 1960): 777-82. Dean was the chairman of the U.S. delegation.

68. Loring, op. cit., p. 406.

69. P.L. 89-658; 80 Stat. 908.

70. Interview with Fellando. Mr. Fellando prefers to term this agreement a "continuation of licensing arrangements" rather than a bilateral agreement.

71. Wolff, op. cit., p. 17.

72. New York Times, July 29, 1956, p. 22 and July 31, 1956, p. 4.

73. New York Times, December 14, 1957, p. 7, December 15, 1957, p. 8, December 19, 1957, p. 2, and January 4, 1958, p. 30. Chile has seized only one vessel. Most of the tuna fishing takes place north of the Chilean claim. Mr. Fellando also considers this a "continuation

of licensing arrangements" rather than a bilateral agreement.

74. Loring, op. cit., pp. 406-07.

75. New York Times, April 14, 1968, sec. 4; Teitelboim, op. cit., p. 43. Loring credits public awareness of this episode as the beginning of Peruvian intransigence on the claim. Since 1965 Peru has demonstrated its leadership repeatedly in spreading and defending the claim.

76. Los Angeles Times, August 17, 1969, p. 2, August 18, 1969, p. 4, and August 20, 1969, p. 11; Teitelboim, op. cit., pp. 53-55.

77. Loring, op. cit., p. 439.

78. New York Times, January 19, 1971, p. 1 and January 20, 1971, p. 10; Los Angeles Times, January 19, 1971, p. 1.

79. OAS/ Official Records / ser. G., CP/SA, 34/71 and ser. G., CP/SA, 38/71. See also New York Times, January 26, 1971, p. 12, January 27, 1971, p. 9, and January 28, 1971, p. 1; Los Angeles Times, January 27, 1971, p. 3 and January 28, 1971, sec. 1.

80. New York Times, January 31, 1971, p. 1.

81. Los Angeles Times, August 31, 1970, p. 6.

82. Robert L. Friedheim, "Understanding the Debate on Ocean Resources," Occasional Paper No. 1 (Kingston, R.I.: The Law of the Sea Institute, February 1969), pp. 44-46, 61.

83. Richard M. Nixon, "U.S. Foreign Policy for the 1970's--The Emerging Structure of Peace: A Report to the Congress," Department of State Bulletin 46, no. 1707 (March 13, 1972), 409-11; Ann L. Hollick, "The Law of the Sea and U.S. Policy Initiatives," Orbis 15, no. 2 (Summer 1971): 670-86.

84. United States: Revised Draft Article on Fisheries (August 4, 1972), Report of the Committee on the Peaceful Uses of the Seabed and the Ocean Floor Beyond the Limits of National Jurisdiction, U.N. General Assembly, Official Records: 27th sess., supp. no. 21 (A/8721).

85. Latin America 5, no. 34 (August 8, 1971).

86. Facts on File, February 25 to March 3, 1973.

87. Colombia-Mexico-Venezuela: Draft Articles for a Treaty on the Territorial Sea (April 2, 1973), International Legal Materials 12, no. 3 (May 1973): 570-72.

88. New York Times, January 7, 1972, p. 2.

3

THE 200-MILE CLAIM
AND LATIN AMERICAN
FOREIGN POLICY

The Latin American claimants would like the 200-mile extension and their defense of it to indicate their greater ability to influence the maritime nations and their growing independence in foreign policy. They have been able to achieve considerable success along these lines, but they have not achieved their primary goal--acceptance of the claim as a legitimate one. The issue remains unresolved and the maritime nations continue to insist that the 200-mile extension is extralegal; because they are unwilling or unable to force a retraction of the claim, the issue is at an impasse. Not all the current claimants of 200-mile zones have made very serious attempts to enforce their claims. This chapter will assess the impact of the claims on the foreign policies of the two nations that have attempted the most vigorous and uniform enforcement of their claims: Ecuador and Peru. In addition we will briefly examine the recent Brazilian claim and the events following it.

The model we will use in assessing these foreign policies originated in James N. Rosenau's works on the relationships--"linkages"--between domestic and foreign policy.[1] He points out that the shrinkage of the world's geographic and social distances with the resultant growth of interdependencies have resulted in the increase of group politics that transcend national boundaries. He says, "Increasingly, therefore, 'internal' events and trends are sustained by 'external' events and trends, so that the distinction between domestic and foreign policy has become increasingly blurred."[2] We believe that the complexities of the fisheries dispute clearly illustrate the influence that group politics can have on foreign policy.

It seems clear that Ecuador and Peru have achieved a
more independent foreign policy with their 20-year defense
of their claims. Peru has even been able to achieve a
leadership role on some issues related to the width of
territorial seas, economic assistance for the less developed nations, and other Third World positions. There are
several reasons for the success that Peruvian and Ecuadorian foreign policies have achieved with their 200-mile
claim.

GROWING SUPPORT FOR THE CLAIMS

In the first place they have made persuasive cases
for the justice, as well as the legality, of their claims.
Their interpretation of international law of the sea as
having been established several centuries ago by customary
agreement to policies acceptable to the major maritime nations is an interpretation that appeals to developing
coastal nations. It coincides not only with their ration-
alizations about their own lack of development, but also
with their prejudices about the avarice of maritime imperialism. In addition the defense of the claims on the
basis of interest in conservation is accepted as an increasingly rational justification. In fact many of the
ecology, conservation, and antipollution concerns are more
acceptable to the developed nations than to the developing
ones. Moreover the fabled untapped and virtually limit-
less wealth of the oceanic food chains is usually recognized today as having been just that: a fable. There
have been too many instances of overfishing and depletion
of certain species. There is also the undeniable evidence
of the despoliation committed on oceanic life because of
pollution from waste disposal and oil spills. The evidence of mercury waste buildup in the fisheries food chain
has convinced the U.S. Food and Drug Administration to
rule on maximum acceptable mercury content in swordfish
and tuna.

INTERNATIONAL BALANCE OF POWERS

Second, the success of the Peruvian and Ecuadorian
foreign policies depends in large measure on the nature
of the international political struggle between the major
world powers--the Soviet Union, China, and the United
States. This competition for allies and influence means

that the use of force or pressure techniques to counter the claims is inadvisable. The days of gunboat diplomacy have ended; sending the fleet to "show the flag" in the Peruvian or Ecuadorian claim zone to demonstrate support for U.S. fishing vessels undoubtedly would be inflammatory and counterproductive.[3] The sentiments of Yankeephobia would interpret such a demonstration of force as heavy-handed U.S. intervention in the policies and independence of Latin America.

U.S. Policy

U.S. policy on the dispute is clouded by conflicting interests. The primary concern of the U.S. Navy in object-ing to the claims has not been aroused by sympathy for the fishing industry; its concern is one of self-interest in "freedom of the seas" in terms of its own navigation and access. Both the Pentagon and the coastal fisheries de-sire maximum control of the waters off the U.S. coasts. The Pentagon and the distant-water fisheries, however, de-sire maximum maneuverability and access to the waters off the coasts of other nations. The U.S. petroleum industry is lobbying for national control of the continental shelves and slopes by all coastal nations.[4] Therefore the mere es-tablishment of a uniform policy on the claims issue is dif-ficult for U.S. policy-makers.

Soviet Policy

To a lesser degree, similar conflicts hamper the po-sition of the Soviet Union on the 200-mile claims.[5] In terms of their advanced trawling techniques, their factory ships, and their widespread fishing activities, the Rus-sians are interested in the narrowest possible territorial seas. They want international law of the sea to enhance freedom of navigation and fishing. For example the Soviet Ministry of Fisheries condemned Argentina's 200-mile exten-sion in 1966 on two grounds. In the first place Argentina had signed all four 1958 Geneva conventions on the law of the sea, but later unilaterally changed its position. Not only was this damaging to the "recognized norms of inter-national law," it was also damaging to the concept of free navigation and fishing on the "high seas."[6] On the other hand, in terms of the extreme anti-Yankee sentiments in Latin America over the claims and continued U.S. fishing, the Soviet Union would like to be able to bolster the claimants, thereby gaining allies and friends. For this reason Soviet fishing vessels buy Argentine fishing licenses.[7]

In addition it must be pointed out that until quite recently the Soviet fishing fleets did not fish off the west coast of South America. Therefore the Soviet government did not come into open conflict with Peru and Ecuador over the 200-mile claim. In 1971, however, the Soviet Union concluded fishing agreements with Peru and Chile. The Peruvian-Soviet agreement provided that the Soviet Union would build a $30 million fishing port at Paita at 3 percent interest, repayable over ten years in fishmeal. Peru made this arrangement in order to expand its facilities for table-food fishing. The agreement provides that an unspecified number of Soviet fishing and research vessels will be based in Peru and allowed to fish in Peruvian waters, conforming to Peruvian laws.[8] The Soviet fisheries minister assured his counterpart in Peru in early 1973 that the Soviet fishing boats would always respect the Peruvian territorial limits.[9]

The public debate in Chile over President Allende's fisheries agreement with the Soviet Union probably means increasing problems for Soviet diplomacy because of her fishing interests. The Soviet-Chilean agreement is basically an agreement by the Chilean government to lease Soviet trawlers in order to increase supplies of fish for human consumption in Chile, to make up for the shortage of beef. It provided that Chile would initially lease three Soviet trawlers, and later eight trawlers and two research vessels, guaranteeing reimbursement of approximately $3.5 million in gold annually. This agreement angered Chilean fishermen and some politicians for several reasons. The introduction of large-scale trawling techniques drew charges that stocks were inadequate and that the resource base was being depleted. It was charged that the Soviet catches were monopolizing Chilean freezer capacity, that they were squeezing out Chilean fishermen, and that, in fact, large quantities of the Soviet catch were going into fishmeal production rather than human consumption. There were also objections to the reimbursement provisions, as well as to the lack of scientific studies preceding the agreement.[10] It seems safe to conclude that the Soviet Union will not be able to engage in sophisticated trawling operations off South America's west coast, even through bilateral fisheries agreements, without arousing the nationalistic, economic, and political concerns of Latin American fishing interests.

China's Policy

The position of China on the 200-mile claim is not complicated by a similar conflict of interests. China has been very sympathetic to the claimants in opposition to both U.S. and Soviet imperialism, as well as in support of the Marxist interpretation of colonialism and economic development. They have been very interested in the widespread Yankeephobia in Latin America; such knowledge has enhanced the Chinese attitude that Latin America is fertile soil for Chinese diplomatic and propaganda efforts.[11] The Peking Review describes the U.S. position on the claims dispute as "imperialism," "gunboat diplomacy," and "piracy."[12] Not only does the dispute give Peking an issue on which she can flay both the United States and the Soviet Union, but China herself feels similarly victimized. Despite bitter Chinese protestations, Japan, Taiwan, and South Korea have licensed international oil companies to drill on the continental shelf of the East China Sea.[13]

Growth of New Nations

Another reason underlying the greater independence of Peruvian and Ecuadorian foreign policy is the growth in sheer numbers of new developing nations. This has given them "ballot power" in the U.N. on issues that unite them against the developed nations. The same ballot power is also true of the OAS. In the case of the latter, however, it is not the growth in numbers of new nations that has created this "us versus U.S." voting configuration. Instead there has been a growth in hemispheric unity as well as in diplomatic skills in structuring certain issues, notably the territorial seas issue, along lines of Latin America versus the United States.

An analysis of U.N. voting patterns on Resolution 2574D of the 24th General Assembly in 1969 is very revealing of these ramifications in a changing world. This particular resolution, sponsored by Latin American nations, proposed a moratorium on all exploitation of the seabed resources outside "national jurisdiction" until an international regime is established. The pre-1969 context of U.N. voting along cold war lines has been replaced by a division of rich nations and poor nations, complicated by patterns of regional voting blocs. The Latin American bloc has become increasingly adept in allying with the Afro-Asian bloc for tactical purposes, and the Soviet bloc shifts according to whether it wants to build rapport with the developing nations or whether it wants a particular substantive goal. The moratorium resolution was passed by a vote of 62 to 28 with 28 abstentions. A number of the abstaining nations have contracted with petroleum companies for offshore drilling. It should be noted that the combination of negative votes and the abstentions divided the General Assembly almost evenly. This division indicates the serious obstacles confronting U.N. attempts to settle the problems of sea and seabed resources.[14]

The extensive experience gained in the repeated defense of the claim has given the Peruvian and Ecuadorian governments the skills and the justification on some issues to become increasingly independent of the United States in the United Nations and the OAS. Peru and Ecuador have not achieved completely independent foreign policies; no "client" nation can do so.[15] Although they are not able to chart consistent Third World courses, the two nations are independent clients. Perhaps the chief significance of the 200-mile claim in their foreign policies is the place it has in their domestic politics. It is an emotional issue pitting David against Goliath in a context that evokes national courage, dignity, and leadership.[16] This kind of national self-image has prompted foreign policy linkages or counterlinkages, which have effectively reinforced David's position while undermining that of Goliath.

PERUVIAN FOREIGN POLICY

Peruvian diplomats have been prominent in promoting the spread of the claim in the case of recent 200-mile extensions proposed in Uruguay and Brazil. They have promoted redefinition of earlier claims in Panama and Argentina. They have encouraged claims in several Latin American nations that have not made them, notably Colombia, Mexico, and Venezuela. According to one expert, the crucial event in this history occurred in 1965 when the details of the secret modus vivendi between Ecuador and the United States became public knowledge. The effect of the secret agreement was a violation of the Declaration of Santiago, which Peru interpreted as evidence of intervention by the Central Intelligence Agency in Latin American politics. The revelation marked the beginning of major intransigence on Peru's part, and Ecuador's part, in maintaining and spreading the claim.[17]

Furthermore, since the 1968 junta's defiance of the United States in expropriating the International Petroleum Company and risking U.S. retaliations, Peru has been charting a new and innovative course in foreign policy. Although the claim and attempts to spread it are not new to Peruvian foreign policy, new active leadership in that realm has been demonstrated. In addition Peru has become more active in Third World politics, particularly in leadership on the law of the sea.

In early 1970, when the United States and the Soviet Union jointly proposed that the U.N. adopt a maximum 12-mile limit of territorial seas and fishery zones, Peru reacted by calling together all the Latin American claimants. The Peruvian foreign minister invited all the claimants to the Montevideo Conference on Latin American Territorial Limits in May 1970 to unify their defense of the 200-mile claim. The Montevideo Conference was followed, a few months later, by a second conference in Lima, which was attended by delegates representing Latin American nations that had not claimed extensions, as well as by observers from African and Asian nations. Fourteen Latin American nations adopted the principle that claims extending territorial waters were justified.[18]

Peru's foreign ministry also has consulted with nations in other parts of the world on the legal, juridical, and foreign policy ramifications of the claims. For example Peru sent a representative to a juridical conference of Afro-Asian nations in Ceylon in early 1971. Naturally Peru strongly supported Ecuador in the Ecuadorian-U.S. confrontation in the OAS in 1971. Peru also has been an active spokesman for the Latin American claimants at the meetings of the U.N. Seabeds Committee since 1970. Parenthetically it should be noted that Venezuela seems to have assumed leadership of the Latin American bloc in the Seabeds Committee, at least among those nations willing to compromise the principle of territoriality.

On other subjects Peru also demonstrated eagerness to engage in a greater leadership role in Third World politics. Peru, along with Chile and Bolivia, vigorously opposed the proposed OAS treaty to deal with hemispheric threats of terrorism by terminating the tradition of political asylum.[19] Peru also has led in the policy determinations of the Andean Pact, headquartered in Lima.[20] Peru lodged energetic protests against the continuation of French nuclear tests in the Pacific in 1971, and France responded by cancelling its last test. In 1972 and 1973,

when France resumed the tests despite Peruvian protests,
Peru threatened again to break off relations with France.[21]

Peru also hosted a meeting of the "Group of 77," which
were actually 95 developing nations, in Lima as a preliminary to the third meeting of the United Nations Congress on
Trade and Development (UNCTAD) in 1972. At this meeting
delegates attempted to formulate unified positions on development to present to the industrial nations. Peru's
leadership (Brazil had led the previous meetings of the
"Group of 77") was demonstrated by its invitation to Cuba
to attend the sessions. More significantly the "Group of
77" affirmed the right of coastal nations to extend their
limits without reference to the 3-mile or 12-mile precedents.[22]

The most revealing evidence of growing independence
in Peru's foreign policy is found in its changing policies
toward the Communist nations--both economically and politically. Peru's first move toward closer relations with the
Soviet bloc began with a trade agreement signed with Hun-
gary in July 1968. Shortly after Peru's 1968 coup, the
new junta government established diplomatic relations with
Rumania promising that this was only the first such move
that they would make. The announcement emphasized Peru's
need to expand trade with the Communist nations. Peru
later signed trade agreements, usually for the sale of
fishmeal, with other Eastern European nations and established formal diplomatic relations with Czechoslovakia and
Yugoslavia. Peru signed a trade agreement with the Soviet
Union in February 1969, only three days following the attempted seizure of the San Juan. Some observers felt that
the attempt on the San Juan may have been timed to reduce
Peruvian criticism of the trade agreement.[23] In the
spring of 1969 formal diplomatic relations were established between Peru and the Soviet Union for the first
time.[24]

Peru and China exchanged trade missions in early 1971.
The head of the first Peruvian trade delegation to China
was the fisheries minister, General Tantalean, who later
concluded a major sale of fishmeal, minerals, and rice to
China. Following these exchanges, in August 1971 Peru announced its intention of extending diplomatic recognition
to China. This also followed the announcement of President Nixon's plans to visit China.

A short time later, in the General Assembly's vote
on the admission of the People's Republic of China, Peru's
growing independence from the tutelage of the United
States became apparent. The first resolution, a U.S.

proposal to label the expulsion of Nationalist China an "important question," thus requiring a two-thirds vote, was defeated 59 to 55 with 15 abstentions. The Latin American nations voting against this resolution included Peru, Ecuador, Chile, Cuba, Guiana, and Trinidad and Tobago. On the Albanian resolution to seat the People's Republic of China and to expel Nationalist China, those same nations voted affirmatively with the addition of Mexico. Four Latin American nations abstained on the latter resolution: Argentina, Barbados, Colombia, and Panama.[25]

Formal relations between Peru and the People's Republic of China were established in November 1971. In the communiqué announcing the formal diplomatic exchange, China recognized Peru's claim to sovereignty over the waters extending 200 miles from its coast. Since then China has become a leading advocate of the Peruvian position on the 200-mile claim in the U.N. Seabeds Committee. Chinese delegates began to attend the meetings of the Seabeds Committee in March 1972. China's outspoken support of the 200-mile claim can be attributed to multiple motives: first, this support reinforces China's claim to be champion of the developing nations; second, China wants to reinforce her own claim to the resources in and under the East China Sea; and third, an internationally accepted 200-mile claim would support Peking's contention that Taiwan belongs to her.[26]

In regard to Cuba several Latin American nations began to reevaluate their relations with Havana as early as 1970. The secretary general of the OAS, Galo Plaza, probed this subject in the hope of accommodating the varying attitudes toward Cuba within the OAS framework. He feared that the new U.S. relationship with China would weaken Latin American "solidarity" and prompt several nations to establish relations with Cuba unilaterally, dealing a severe blow to the inter-American system. Therefore he discussed the issue with representatives of Mexico, Peru, Chile, Ecuador, Colombia, Uruguay, Bolivia, and Costa Rica. All reportedly favored normalizing relations with Cuba. Other members, including the United States, Brazil, Argentina, Guatemala, the Dominican Republic, and Venezuela, opposed easing sanctions against Cuba.[27]

The outcome of the OAS discussions was the secretary general's appointment of a committee in December 1971 to study the lifting of sanctions against Cuba. The plan also allowed OAS member nations, on Peru's request, to establish individual diplomatic and trade relations with Cuba. Reportedly both Peru and Ecuador were eager to be the first nation to request the OAS to remove its 1964 sanctions against Cuba.[28] Peru and Cuba did reestablish formal diplomatic relations in 1972.[29]

Finally it must be pointed out that Peruvian diplomacy under the junta's foreign minister, General Edgardo Mercado Jarrin, has been skillfully handled and extremely effective. Despite the innovations of Peruvian foreign policy, Peru has had remarkably good relations with the United States. For example the Hickenlooper Amendment, which calls for suspension of U.S. aid if nationalized U.S. companies are not promptly and adequately compensated, was never applied in retaliation to the nationalization of the International Petroleum Company. Naturally these good relations with the United States must be credited to the U.S. efforts to reduce hemispheric tensions with "low profile" policies, as well as to the skillful diplomacy of the Peruvian foreign ministry. In addition it must be pointed out that Peruvian leadership of Latin American development strategy has increased the costs of U.S. confrontation with the junta.[30] Peru also has maintained good relations with such conservative Latin American governments as those of Ecuador and Brazil. Obviously the 200-mile claim is the issue of their greatest unity.

ECUADORIAN FOREIGN POLICY

Ecuador's foreign policy is not as distinctive as that of Peru. The Ecuadorian government is considerably more conservative than the Peruvian junta. Ecuador has not been willing or able to attempt the kind of influence in Third World politics that characterizes recent Peruvian foreign policy. This is not to say that Ecuador's foreign policy has not shown innovative leadership on occasion.

In 1967 Ecuador abstained on the annual General Assembly vote on the question of seating the People's Republic of China, and she continued to abstain in 1968, 1969, and 1970. Therefore Ecuador's leadership in the 1971 debates on the question did not develop out of hasty considerations. Ecuador's delegate to the United Nations, Leopoldo Benitez, made a definitive speech early in the 1971 debate. He formulated arguments of jurisprudence that were appealing to the other Latin American supporters of Peking. Benitez noted that to argue that Chiang Kai-shek's government should remain in the United Nations because it had signed the Charter 26 years earlier was like saying the United Nations had "personal contracts" with individual heads of state. He maintained that the question was not one of depriving a member state of representation, but one

of deciding whether Peking or Taipei was the "lawful representative of the people of China."[31] Ecuador does not have
diplomatic relations with China, but the two nations have
exchanged trade delegations.

Ecuador and the Soviet Union made their first trade
agreement in 1970. The Soviet Union contracted to buy
10,000 tons of bananas and expected to increase that purchase by an additional 15,000 tons in 1971.[32] In early 1971
Ecuador and the Soviet Union also exchanged formal diplomatic recognition. Ambassador Marchuk, the new Soviet ambassador to Ecuador, discovered at his first press conference
that the 200-mile claim would require very skillful diplomacy on his part. The Soviet Union would like to exploit the
200-mile issue to its advantage in much the same manner as
the Chinese diplomats have been able to exploit it. This is
difficult because the Latin American claimants recognize the
hypocrisy of such support in the face of both the Soviet adherence to a 12-mile zone and the extensive Soviet fishing in
several oceans. Currently there is no Soviet fishing off the
Ecuadorian coast.

Ambassador Marchuk opened his first press conference in
Guayaquil by pointedly praising Ecuadorian bananas and promising increased Soviet purchase of bananas. The Ecuadorian
officials and press representatives were more interested,
however, in questioning the Soviet attitude toward the 200-
mile claim. The ambassador was evasive, replying that such
claims must be determined multilaterally rather than unilaterally. He did point out that the USSR did not apply sanctions nor "invade" Ecuadorian territorial waters as the United States does. El Comercio condemned the Soviet diplomat
editorially for his "diplomatic pirouettes" and charged that
Russia was aligned with the great industrial fishing nations,
Japan and the United States. For this reason the editorial
urged the developing nations to unite in order to hold back
the fleets of the more powerful nations.[33]

Ecuador's relations with the United States have been
handled adroitly, most notably in maneuvering the 1971
seizures-sanctions dispute into the special session of the
OAS Council. The council, despite urgent U.S. objections,
voted 22 to 0 with U.S. abstention, to take up Ecuador's
charge of "economic coercion." This vote signified a kind
of hemispheric "moral support." The later compromise resolution calling for the United States and Ecuador to negotiate their differences passed by a vote of 19 to 0 with
four abstentions. At first Ecuador declared that this was
an important symbolic victory for her. Shortly afterward,
however, Ecuador apparently decided it was not enough of a
victory and expelled the U.S. military missions.

47

It must be noted that the U.S. arms-sales ban was just that and nothing more--it would not have meant the U.S. withdrawal of its military missions. The Pentagon's long-held position has been to retain military missions throughout Latin America in order to promote U.S. influence over officers and weapons procurement. U.S. military assistance affected by the sales ban and expulsion of the missions was about $2 million annually. Specifically, in 1971 the estimated dollar value of suspended arms sales was $1,271,000. In addition the missions administered about $500,000 annually in training expenditures.[34]

It may be that Ecuador's foreign policy in escalating the seizures and fines has forced at least partial acceptance of the reality, if not the legality of the claim. Some 30 U.S. tuna boats were reported to have purchased Ecuadorian <u>matriculas</u> or entry permits. These preliminary documents cost $350 each; they allow a vessel to first locate fish and then to apply by radio for an Ecuadorian license.[35] Other reports claimed 15 U.S. vessels purchased licenses before sailing into the Ecuadorian claim zone.[36] The ATA denies, however, that there has been any significant increase in license purchases.

Ecuador's foreign policy has been able to avoid harsher retaliations against its seizures because of the complexities of its own and U.S. economic interests. For example the U.S. tuna industry urged an embargo on Ecuadorian products and, in fact, in 1971 staged a brief picket line halting the unloading of a cargo of Ecuadorian bananas. Ironically the bananas were owned by a U.S. corporation and were loaded in a German vessel.[37]

Although there are significant U.S. investments in Ecuadorian bananas, the development of a newly discovered oil field in Ecuador's Oriente east of the Andes is of considerably greater importance to U.S. investors than either bananas or tuna. The oil field is the first natural resource of tremendous value to be found in Ecuador. It is called an oil "trap" with vast deposits of high-quality, sulfur-free petroleum, which means that it will not require costly double refining to meet U.S. antipollution standards. Rumors refer to the find as "another Venezuela." In fact exaggerated predictions for the field's productivity place it as high as five million barrels a day by 1975--half of current U.S. production and greater than Venezuelan production of 3.7 million barrels a day.[38] Ecuador's own Ministry of National Resources and Tourism makes a more conservative estimate of 75,000 barrels a day by 1976.

Gulf and Texaco joined in a consortium to construct a pipeline across the Andes. Production began in 1972 and provided for vast increases in Ecuador's foreign exchange earnings. It is crucial to note that during the 1971 "tuna war," an agreement on the profits split between the U.S.-owned consortium and the Ecuadorian government had not been signed. Furthermore, with the cuts in U.S. assistance, the hard-pressed Ecuadorian government demanded and got "advance royalties" from the consortium.

This apparently did not upset the oil companies as much as the implicit threat to reduce the consortium's share of profits. The oil men were very concerned that every seizure incident stimulated the Ecuadorian index of nationalism, probably reducing their share in the forthcoming profit split. Consequently the oil companies lobbied vigorously for Washington to reduce tensions over the fishing dispute for the companies' sake.[39] They argue that they have at stake many times the value of the tuna caught by U.S. vessels in the Ecuadorian claim area. The authors believe that this argument is at least one reason for the inflated figures for the value of the Ecuadorian oil fields mentioned above. This is indicative of the pressure, or linkage, the oil industry has levered in an attempt to get the State Department to settle the fishing dispute so that delicate oil negotiations would not be disrupted. The annual catch of the U.S. tuna fleet in the Pacific is worth some $70 million--in 1970 the total cash value of the catch was $74,733,000. Because fishing patterns for tuna vary from year to year, the estimates of the value of the fish caught in the waters claimed by Ecuador vary from $5 million to $25 million.[40]

It is of major concern and real economic need for Ecuador to have the oil resources developed. With rampant nationalistic phobias about foreign imperialists who devour Latin American resources, such development must be achieved without seeming to bend to the whims of the foreign exploiters. The fishing boat seizures provide multifaceted linkages or counterlinkages to apply toward this goal. The seizures allow the Ecuadorian government to grant concessions to foreign petroleum companies without being accused of "selling out" to foreign imperialists.

In addition it appears that the oil industry's pressure may compel the State Department to negotiate the claims dispute on the kind of terms that Ecuador wants. During bilateral U.S.-Ecuadorian talks in late 1971 and early 1972, State Department representatives proposed that they request congressional authorization for license purchase "under protest" in return for guaranteed "free

transit" in the waters and air space beyond 12 miles.
Ecuador rejected this and other proposals because of her
refusal to negotiate the dispute while the United States'
retaliatory legislation remains in effect.[41] Consequently
such a measure has not been introduced in Congress. However, there has been an increasing number of Congressmen
who have indicated that the U.S. government would save
money by purchasing fishing licenses for the tuna boats
rather than reimbursing the fines and costs of seizure.

State Department representatives have appeared regu-
larly before congressional committees in opposition to retaliatory legislative proposals. Recently, however, they
have pointed to the specific counterproductivity of the
retaliatory fishing legislation in escalating the rate of
seizures and the punitiveness of the fines. In addition
they point out that such laws may damage other U.S. economic interests--oil, bananas, fishmeal, minerals--as well
as diplomatic relationships within the hemisphere.[42]

Although the linkages of the petroleum industry are
the most significant economic pressures affecting the
claims dispute, the most paradoxical linkages are the U.S.
investments in Ecuadorian fisheries. U.S. businesses own
or control a large share of Ecuador's tuna fleet and two
fish canneries in Ecuador. Reportedly more than 50 percent of Ecuador's annual 35,000-ton tuna catch was processed by subsidiaries of two U.S. companies, Del Monte
and Stokeley-Van Camp. Each firm ships up to 6,000 tons
of frozen tuna from Ecuador to U.S. packers annually.
Furthermore both companies have investments in the Ecuadorian tuna fleet, more than half of which is U.S.-owned
or U.S.-financed. On hearing of the dual involvement of
U.S. private interests in the "tuna war," a Florida congressman wondered if private investments were not guiding
U.S. policy in the "game" they were playing, with "U.S.
citizens fighting among themselves for money."[43] Regardless of whether the U.S. investments in the Ecuadorian
tuna industry are more beneficial to Ecuador or to the
U.S. investors, they complicate diplomatic solution of
the claims dispute. Private U.S. investments not only
have conflicts of interests affecting the dispute, but
within the U.S. tuna industry itself there are dual and
overlapping interests in the Ecuadorian claim.

LINKAGES AND THE 200-MILE CLAIM

An obvious linkage is the continuation and expansion
of the increasingly efficient U.S. tuna industry's producing goods for a very attractive market. This linkage

has several ramifications. In the first place it means
that Ecuador and Peru see the tuna clippers as "penetra-
tors" and invaders. The offshore extensions meant that
attempts to enforce the claims were requisite if they were
not honored. Therefore counterlinkages of seizures and
fines occurred. Originally both Peru and Ecuador hoped to
persuade the tuna canneries and fleets to relocate their
bases in Peru or Ecuador, providing investment capital and
employment for their citizens. In Ecuador's case, as discussed above, the fledgling tuna industry is dominated by
U.S. subsidiaries. In the case of Peru this pattern has
not developed. However, in the light of the economic incentives provided by Peru's new General Fisheries Law (see
Chapter 4), some facets of the U.S. tuna industry might
establish canneries and fleets in Peru.

Another reaction to the attractive world market for
tuna has been the entry of other nations into the race for
tuna. Several governments, especially Japan, South Korea,
Taiwan, and Canada, have subsidized tuna boat construction.
This sort of unlimited entry has been typical in many fisheries because of the common-property nature of the resource. It almost always results in two patterns: uneconomic fishing and depleted resources. Because of the migratory nature of tuna and the attractive tuna market, the
Latin American efforts to nationalize and regulate the resource have been to little avail.

Another linkage has been the withholding or the
threatened withholding of several varieties of U.S. assistance, or other punitive actions, in retaliation for the
seizures. These linkages have led to a variety of reac-
tions in the affected nations--all of them escalatory.
Sometimes they have meant more seizures and higher fines;
sometimes they have meant the discontinuation or the
threatened discontinuation of negotiations on the dispute.
Both Ecuador and Peru have expelled U.S. military missions
because of arms-sales suspensions. Ecuador's response to
the 1971 arms-sales ban was to charge the United States
with "economic coercion," which gained important symbolic
hemispheric support in the OAS Council.

Perhaps the most intricate evidence of linkages is
found in the conflicting, overlapping dual interests of
U.S. economic and political sectors in Latin America.
The tuna industry attempted to exert linkage pressure by
urging boycotts and embargoes on Ecuadorian and Peruvian
products. They discovered that these efforts are potentially damaging to other U.S. investments in Latin America.
It may be assumed that the U.S. interests in bananas or in
minerals feel some gratitude toward the tuna clippers for

taking the heat off them in the past few years. That gratitude evaporates, however, with the threat of boycott or
embargo of their products. In addition to the U.S. investments in the claimant nations, there are also U.S. interests profiting by export sales to the claimants. For example the United States had a favorable balance of trade
with Ecuador in 1970 of about $25 million, exporting prod-
ucts worth about $96 million while importing about $73
million worth of Ecuadorian products.[44] In addition the
U.S. fish canneries located in Puerto Rico depend partly
on imports of frozen fish from Ecuador and Peru for their
fish supplies. Also, among large-scale U.S. farmers there
is widespread use of protein supplements--often Peruvian
fishmeal--for poultry and livestock feed.

The counterlinkage pressures exercised by Ecuador on
the U.S. oil consortium apparently have induced the State
Department to make the sort of offer that might be acceptable to the claimants. Despite the State Department's 20-
year position against voluntary license purchase because
it implies de facto recognition of the 200-mile claim, the
State Department tentatively suggested to Ecuador that it
propose legislation providing for official license purchase in return for navigational access beyond 12 miles.
The U.S. Navy remains implacably opposed to these compromise proposals or to any others that hint at implied ap-
proval of the 200-mile claim. It remains to be seen
whether the Pentagon or the State Department will determine this policy. From the viewpoint of linkage theory,
however, it is instructive to note that this compromise
was proposed by the State Department only after Ecuador
was able to apply strong counterlinkages to the powerful
U.S. petroleum industry.

There are still other linkage patterns in the dispute. The reimbursement of fines and the other costs of
seizures, as provided by the Fishermen's Protective Acts,
means that almost all financial costs of the seizures are
subsidized by U.S. taxpayers. This practice removes the
financial risk of the seizures, and does little to promote the sale of licenses. It has even been alleged that
the 1967 legislation has made it possible for skippers to
make money from a seizure. If a catch is confiscated,
the owners can be reimbursed for half its value, according to a vessel's own estimate of the quantity seized,
leaving room for padded estimates of confiscated catches.[45]

Other linkages include the U.S. military assistance
programs to the Ecuadorian and Peruvian navies for vessel
loans, military sales, and the U.S. tariffs on tuna imports.

The 1969 Ecuadorian law that grants Ecuador's Navy 70 percent of the total fines collected is a clear example of a
fused linkage.

In addition to the linkages in the disputes over
Peruvian and Ecuadorian claims, we will briefly examine
the linkages connected with Brazil's recent claim.   In
this case they are readily apparent and condensed in time.
The Brazilian claim to 200 miles, decreed in March 1970,
became effective June 1, 1971 with a unique law that di-
vides the 200 miles into two separate zones.   The first
100 miles are reserved for Brazilian vessels and the second 100 miles may be fished by licensed foreign vessels.
The law prohibits foreign vessels from fishing for shellfish, although this prohibition can be alleviated by re-
locating in Brazil or by the home country's negotiation
of a licensing agreement with Brazil.

Initially the State Department announced that the 400
to 500 U.S.-owned shrimp boats, many of which are based in
French Guiana, Surinam, and Trinidad and Tobago, would not
buy licenses.[46]   The House of Representatives was even
more intransigent; it delayed action on the international
coffee agreement.   The Brazilian note of protest, in fact,
even used the term "link":   "we are not prepared to accept
any connection between this matter and the extension of
Brazilian territorial waters, and any attempt to link the
two matters would be considered as intolerable economic
pressure on a matter concerning the sovereignty of the
Brazilian state."[47]

Brazil retaliated by suspending the soluble coffee
agreement it had maintained with the United States.   This
agreement allowed U.S. firms to buy a maximum of 500,000
bags of coffee per year free of the export tax--a provision which put them on the same footing as Brazilian ex-
porters--in return for the elimination of U.S. import
duties on Brazilian soluble coffee.[48]   Brazil also made
it clear that she intended to enforce the claim.   On June
16, 1971, a Brazilian gunboat fired warning shots at an
American shrimp boat, then circled it and other shrimp
boats for several hours.[49]   Moreover the speeches and
statements by Brazilian naval authorities manifested a
more aggressive attitude.[50]

On May 9, 1972, the United States and Brazil signed
an agreement on shrimping to last until January 1, 1974,
when it was renewed because there is still no international agreement on the width of territorial seas.   This
agreement is basically a conservation agreement for shrimp,
a relatively sedentary crustacean.   Its terms reduced the

number of U.S. shrimp boats, previously 400 to 500, to 325. This is the first effort of U.S. policy to reduce participants in a fishery. These vessels will purchase licenses and keep logs for quarterly delivery to Brazilian fishery authorities for the compilation of statistical conservation data. Only 160 U.S. vessels will be allowed to fish at any one time. There are also prohibitions against certain kinds of illegal fishing gear, chemicals, and explosives, as well as against fishing in spawning grounds. The agreement stipulates that it is an interim solution to shrimping conservation "without prejudice to either Party's juridical position concerning the extent of territorial seas or fisheries jurisdiction under international law." The most interesting feature of the agreement is the seemingly paradoxical provision that the United States will compensate Brazil $200,000 annually for patrolling and enforcing the agreement. The United States also will pay Brazil $100 for each day she holds a U.S.-flag vessel for violation of the agreement.[51] Furthermore Brazil reportedly considered purchase of British or French aircraft to patrol the coastal waters, a very skillful practice of linkage politics.[52]

Some observers believe that the U.S.-Brazilian agreement may become a model for U.S. agreements with the CEP nations. Privately the United States has suggested that a Brazilian-type agreement might be worked out with Ecuador. Presumably the U.S. tuna boats would purchase licenses, perhaps reimbursed by the U.S. government, with the understanding that such purchase grants no tacit recognition of the 200-mile claim. The boatowners oppose license purchase, fearing that the practice would spread inevitably to all the nations in whose shores the vessels fish or sail. Since this involves possibly nine nations in the eastern Pacific alone, the ATA believes the burden of license purchase would be prohibitive.

In conclusion we believe the Latin American claimants have been able to develop more independent foreign policies in recent years. It is clear that this growth in independence is the result of two factors. In the first place, as Sergio Teitelboim points out, there is an aspect of "continental nationalism" and a "new mentality" demonstrated by the maintenance of the claims. The claimants recognize the contradictions between the United States and Latin America and are determined to avoid a subordinate position to tutelary U.S. policy.[53] Second, it is clear that the growth of more independent foreign policies is a result of the pressures these policies are able to exert because of the growth of global interdependencies. Neither Ecuador nor Peru nor Brazil is helpless when it comes to having an impact on the policies of the major maritime nations, including the United States. The linkages produced by the increase of mutual interdependencies have enabled these nations to become increasingly independent in their foreign policies. It is obvious that the distinctions between dependence, interdependence, and independence have diminished in the Latin American fisheries dispute.

NOTES

1. James N. Rosenau, "Toward the Study of National-International Linkages," in Linkage Politics: Essays on the Convergence of National and International Systems, ed. James N. Rosenau (New York: The Free Press, 1969), pp. 44-63; James N. Rosenau, The Scientific Study of Foreign Policy (New York: The Free Press, 1971), pp. 127-30. It is also instructive to note other studies of Latin American politics that have used Rosenau's concepts. See Carlos Alberto Astiz, Pressure Groups and Power Elites in Peruvian Politics (Ithaca: Cornell University Press, 1969), chap. 10; Richard B. Craig, The Bracero Program: Interest Groups and Foreign Policy (Austin: University of Texas Press, 1971); Yale H. Ferguson, "Introduction," in Contemporary Inter-American Relations: A Reader in Theory and Issues, ed. Yale H. Ferguson (Englewood Cliffs, N.J.: Prentice-Hall, 1972), pp. 1-7; Douglas A. Chalmers, "Developing on the Periphery: External Factors in Latin American Politics," in Rosenau, Linkage Politics, op. cit., pp. 67-93; Rod Bunker, "Linkages and the Foreign Policy of Peru, 1958-1966," Western Political Quarterly 22, no. 2 (June 1969): 280-97; and Carlos Alberto Astiz, "The Latin American Countries in the International System," in Latin American International Politics, ed. Carlos Alberto Astiz (Notre Dame, Ind.: University of Notre Dame Press, 1969), pp. 3-17.

2. James N. Rosenau, "Adaptive Polities in an Interdependent World," Orbis 16, no. 1 (Spring 1972): 156.

3. Neale Ronning, Law and Politics in Inter-American Diplomacy (New York: John Wiley, 1963), p. 121.

4. John A. Knauss, "Factors Influencing a U.S. Position in a Future Law of the Sea Conference," Occasional Paper No. 10 (Kingston, R.I.: The Law of the Sea Institute, April 1970).

5. Margaret Lynch Gerstle, "The Politics of UN Voting: A View of the Seabed from the Glass Palace," Occasional Paper No. 7 (Kingston, R.I.: The Law of the Sea Institute, July 1970), p. 9.

6. "U.S.S.R. Ministry of Fisheries Article on Freedom of High Seas," International Legal Materials 8 (1969): 896-98. See also W. Joseph Dehner, "Creeping Jurisdiction in the Arctic: Has the Soviet Union Joined Canada?" Harvard International Law Journal 13, no. 2 (Spring 1972): 276-77.

7. David C. Loring, "The United States-Peruvian 'Fisheries' Dispute," Stanford Law Review 23, no. 3 (February 1971): 452.

8. Peru-Union of Soviet Socialist Republics: Agreement on Cooperation for the Development of the Fishing Industry, Lima, September 4, 1971, International Legal Materials 11 (1972): 304-08.

9. Latin America 7, no. 5 (February 2, 1973).

10. Chile-Union of Soviet Socialist Republics: Contract for the Use of Soviet Vessels for Fishing Operations, Moscow, December 7, 1971, International Legal Materials 11 (1972): 947-51; "Chile: Senate Discussion of the Chile-Union of Soviet Socialist Republics Contract for the Use of Soviet Vessels for Fishing Operations," International Legal Materials 11 (1972): 1156-58; Los Angeles Times, April 16, 1972, p. 7.

11. Cecil Johnson, Communist China and Latin America, 1959-1967 (New York: Columbia University Press, 1970).

12. "Support Latin American Countries' Struggle to Defend Their Territorial Sea Rights" and "Latin American Countries Ranged Against U.S. Imperialist Aggression to Defend Their Territorial Sea Rights," Peking Review 48 (November 27, 1970): 7-10.

13. "People's Republic of China Statement on the Law of the Sea," made at the UN Committee on the Peaceful Uses of the Seabed, March 3, 1972, International Legal Materials 11 (1972): 654-61. See also Choon-Ho Park, "Oil Under Troubled Waters: The Northeast Asia Seabed Controversy," Harvard International Law Journal 14, no. 2 (Spring 1973): 212-60; Latin America 5, no. 2 (January 8, 1971): and New York Times, March 20, 1972, p. 13.

14. Gerstle, op. cit., pp. 2-4.

15. Norman A. Bailey, Latin America in World Politics (New York: Walker and Company, 1967), pp. 150-57.

16. Virginia M. Hagen, "The Latin American-United States Fishing Rights Controversy: Dilemma for United States Foreign Policy (1969-1971)," Congressional Research

Service, Library of Congress, April 15, 1971. Reprinted
in House of Representatives, Committee on Foreign Affairs,
Subcommittee on Inter-American Affairs, Fishing Rights and
United States-Latin American Relations, 92d Cong., 2d sess.,
1972, pp. 98-99.

17. Loring, op. cit., pp. 392, 407-09.

18. New York Times, May 10, 1970, p. 14 and August
16, 1970, p. 21.

19. Latin America 5, no. 8 (February 19, 1971).

20. Latin America 5, no. 38 (September 17, 1971).

21. New York Times, August 26, 1971, p. 16; Latin
America 5, no. 38 (September 17, 1971).

22. Latin America 6, no. 22 (June 2, 1972).

23. Loring, op. cit., p. 433; New York Times, February 18, 1969, p. 1.

24. New York Times, February 2, 1969, p. 4.

25. Facts on File 31, no. 1617, October 21-October
27, 1971.

26. New York Times, March 20, 1972, p. 13.

27. Facts on File 31, no. 1609, August 26-September
1, 1971.

28. Facts on File 31, no. 1624, December 9-December
15, 1971.

29. Facts on File 32, no. 1661, August 26-September
2, 1972.

30. New York Times, October 20, 1971, p. 1.

31. Wall Street Journal, December 6, 1970, p. 21.

32. New York Times, March 28, 1971, p. 23.

33. Hagen, op. cit., p. 84.

34. New York Times, January 7, 1972, p. 2.

35. Los Angeles Times, February 6, 1972, sec. C.

36. Los Angeles Times, March 16, 1971, sec. I.

37. New York Times, July 18, 1971, sec. 3.

38. New York Times, May 17, 1971, p. 53; July 18,
1971, sec. 3; and January 30, 1972, sec. 3.

39. U.S. House of Representatives, Committee on Foreign Affairs, Subcommittee on Inter-American Affairs,
Hearings on Fishing Rights and United States-Latin American
Relations, 92d Cong., 2d sess., February 3, 1972, pp. 13-
14, 23.

40. Ibid., pp. 10-11; and New York Times, January
30, 1972, sec. 3.

41. U.S. House of Representatives, Committee on
Merchant Marine, Subcommittee on Fisheries and Wildlife
Conservation, Hearings on Illegal Seizures, 92d Cong.,
1st sess., 1971, p. 113; and Hearings on Fishing Rights
and United States-Latin American Relations, op. cit., pp.
4-29.

42. Hearings on Fishing Rights and United States-Latin American Relations, op. cit., p. 25.

43. Hearings on Illegal Seizures, op. cit., p. 131.

44. New York Times, January 30, 1972, sec. 3. This article was written by H. J. Maidenburg.

45. New York Times, June 6, 1971, p. 12.

46. Latin America 5, no. 25 (June 18, 1971).

47. Latin America 5, no. 30 (July 23, 1971).

48. Los Angeles Times, June 17, 1971, p. 4.

49. Latin America 6, no. 10 (March 10, 1972) and 6, no. 12 (March 24, 1972).

50. Agreement Between the Government of the Federative Republic of Brazil and the Government of the United States of America Concerning Shrimp, U.S. Department of State, Press Release no. 111, May 9, 1972.

51. Latin America 6, no. 23 (June 9, 1972).

52. Rosenau, "Adaptive Polities in an Interdependent World," op. cit., pp. 153-73.

53. Sergio Teitelboim, "Los países del Pacífico Sur y el mar territorial," Estudios Internacionales 4, no. 3 (April-June 1970): 53.

Peruvian economic history has largely been told in
the past by the rise and decline of several booms--silver,
copper, guano, sugar, and cotton. While they are indicative of Peru's varied geography, these booms were all
characterized by the patterns of the classic enclave-
export economy. Enclave economies are heavily dependent
on the export of raw materials or extractive commodities,
ordinarily derived from mining or agriculture. Typically
these products are confined to relatively restricted areas
and are produced by relatively few producers; thus they
have very little impact on the rest of the economy. Enclave economies are dual economies, in which foreign-
owned enterprises usually dominate the extractive export
industry, while much of the rest of the economy stagnates
or is outside of a monetary economy entirely. The enclave economy is also characterized by heavy dependence
on price fluctuations in the world market. Latin American economic history in general, as well as Peruvian history, is replete with examples of the boom-and-bust cycles.
That is, a raw material moved abruptly to the center of
the economic stage attracting planters, surveyors, foreign
capitalists, speculators, and hangers-on, all eager to

The authors have written two articles on similar subjects. See "Fishmeal and the Peruvian Economy," The Quarterly Review of Economics and Business 10, no. 3 (Autumn
1970): 35-45, and "Peruvian Fisheries: Conservation and
Development," Journal of Economic Development and Cultural
Change 21, no. 2 (January 1972).

plant new land or open new mines; the boom contagion was then followed by a price collapse a short time later, either because of overproduction or the introduction of substitute products or competition from other enclave economies elsewhere.[1]

In the decade of the mid-1950s to the mid-1960s Peru struck it rich again; this time the Humboldt Current was mined for anchovies. The resultant fishmeal boom propelled Peru into the position of being the world's leading exporter of fish in 1962, surpassing even Japan. Peru has held that position every year since (see Table 1). This achievement was due almost exclusively to harvesting the abundant anchovy resource and refining it, in a relatively simple process, into fishmeal. The purpose of this chapter is to investigate the fishmeal boom and assess its impact on the Peruvian economic and political system. In particular we will be interested in seeing whether Peruvian fishmeal is typical of the enclave-export economies described above, or whether it has stimulated much basic economic development.

TABLE 1

Exports of Peruvian Fishery Products, 1958-70

Year	Amount (metric tons)
1958	146,513.5
1959	352,567.7
1960	592,229.7
1961	865,042.5
1962	1,232,781.9
1963	1,212,827.7
1964	1,574,736.1
1965	1,582,805.0
1966	1,426,176.3
1967	1,816,950.8
1968	2,419,888.0
1969	1,901,247.1
1970	2,103,948.6
1971	2,045,000.0
1972	1,832,000.0

Sources: Anuario de Pesca, 1970-1971, pp. 196-97; for 1971 and 1972: Peruvian Times, July 27, 1973, p. 2.

Interest in the fishmeal boom is heightened by the realization that the same resource was also involved in one of Peru's previous boom cycles, one, in fact, which is a classic example of the nature of the enclave-export economy--the guano industry. For centuries the millions of birds along the dry Peruvian coast fed on anchovies and deposited their manure, guano, on uninhabited coastal islands. Even though the Incas had known the value of guano as fertilizer, the Spanish, lured by more lustrous minerals, failed to develop this resource.

The Peruvian Republic began exploitation of guano in the mid-nineteenth century by selling guano consignments to British and French corporations, giving the consignee the exclusive right to sell guano in a designated area.[2] Desperately needing revenues, the government borrowed large sums of money as advances to be repaid by future guano sales. For several decades it was a very lucrative enterprise: Chinese coolies were sometimes indentured for years extracting guano at very low cost;[3] and the agricultural demand for the fertilizer was very heavy. The boom ended rather abruptly for several reasons: competition from other fertilizers, especially Chilean and Bolivian nitrates; the depletion of the major guano deposits; and Peru's disastrous defeat in the War of the Pacific (1879-83). Peru's desire to protect her guano industry had stimulated her own interest in the coastal nitrates--she hoped to backstop guano prices by manipulating those of the newer fertilizer. Chile's reaction was to take nitrate-producing lands claimed by both Peru and Bolivia; Chile, in fact, occupied Peru's major guano islands temporarily, felicitously promoting her own nitrate boom.

The impact of the guano boom on the Peruvian economy has been depicted by Jonathan Levin as a classic example of the enclave economy. He finds that possibly half the income from the guano trade went to the Peruvian government, whose expenditures did little to promote real economic development. Part of the income was lost through corruption and high interest rates; some of it went to finance particular political goals--freeing the Negro slaves, modernization of Lima's public utilities, and eliminating, or greatly reducing, taxes. Levin concludes, however, that most of the government's guano income went to promote the narrow interests of those in control; he characterizes the expanded numbers of bureaucrats, militarists, and pensioners as "empleomania." These recipients of the guano income were "luxury importers" who conspicuously consumed imported luxury items, or invested in

still another enclave economy: the new Peruvian sugar industry. The only basic expenditure that was an exception
was for railroad construction, which had a delayed impact
on the Peruvian economy.[4] The economy remained basically
so inactive, with expenditures so conspicuous and revenues
so bound to an extractive product, that Peru remained in a
state of arrested development when the guano was depleted.
Other writers have described the Peruvian guano economy as
"an economic windfall rather than a self-sustaining economy"[5] and as a "semi-modern" or "partial industrial" economy.[6]

FISHMEAL BOOM

Fishmeal is a protein that accelerates growth when
fed in controlled amounts to livestock. It is used ex-
tensively for poultry in the developed countries. An estimated 90 percent of all fishmeal consumed goes to bal-
anced poultry feeds, with no more than 10 percent of the
mixture being fishmeal. Hog rations use the remaining 10
percent of fishmeal. Cattle reject the odor of fishmeal.[7]
In terms of proteins fishmeal fed to poultry produces
amino acids and nutritional value that are identical to
those of the favored fish species in the diets of the in-
dustrialized nations. Such improvement can be provided
at less than one-thirtieth of the cost of salmon or tuna.[8]
The fact remains, however, that these proteins are ex-
tracted from the "hungry" nations suffering from protein
shortages for the benefit of the well-fed world.[9]
Fishmeal is produced relatively simply. Anchovies
travel in shoals, enabling them to be captured by surrounding the shoals with a net and hauling them in on
small purse seiners called <u>bolicheras</u>. The catch is transferred from the boat to the fishmeal plant by means of
fish pumps. It is cooked for about 25 minutes in steam
cookers, followed by pressing. The pulp goes into a dryer
while the liquid goes to centrifuges that separate the
fishoil from water. The remaining liquid, stickwater, was
discarded in the early years of the industry. Now, in the
more efficient plants, stickwater is pumped into a stickwater plant where the liquids are evaporated, leaving
solid proteins, which are added to the dryer. Antioxi-
dants are sprayed onto the fishmeal, which is then ground
and sometimes pelletized. The finished product is stored
for 21 days before loading in order to further control the
oxidation process. The chemical combination of unsaturated

fat, water, and oxygen created considerable danger of spon-
taneous combustion and shipboard fires before the producers
learned to control the rate of oxidation.

The development of the first Peruvian fishmeal plant
was a direct outgrowth of fish canneries; the reduction of
fishmeal was started in order to use the waste materials
from canned bonito and tuna. Soon whole anchovies were
being processed as well. Because of the historical importance of guano, fishmeal production began in virtual
secrecy. By the mid-1950s, however, the objections of the
guano industry could raise no more than very temporary
obstacles to the boom. In 1956 the guano monopoly pressed
the government to temporarily decree a halt in fishmeal
plant construction until further studies could be made of
the effects on the bird population. This decree was lifted
in 1959 and marked a key defeat for the guano industry.[10]
Guano production has dropped drastically since the fishmeal
boom began in earnest. In 1956, 330,000 tons of guano were
produced; in 1970 only 51,679 tons were produced.[11] It
should be noted that during the height of the guano boom,
the annual harvest from the three richest guano islands
alone was some 400,000 tons annually.[12]

Since the fishmeal industry was destined to override
the protestations of the guano industry, an even more important year in the history of the fishmeal boom was 1956,
when nylon nets were introduced. The cotton nets used
earlier were very short-lived and heavy when wet, thus
raising a considerable cost barrier to expansion. Nylon
nets had many advantages: they were much less affected by
mildew and rot, and were stronger and lighter than cotton
and lasted much longer. Furthermore their lightness and
strength allowed for the introduction of larger boats.
Michael Roemer's study of the industry reports that the
major expansion of the fishmeal industry came as a result
of this technological advance.[13]

The boom is reflected in the rapid expansion of the
number of fishmeal reduction plants along the Peruvian
coast. At one time there were more than 170 separate
plants. There has been considerable variation, however,
in the number of plants in operation during a given year.
In some years plants shut down for several reasons: scar-
city of fish in the vicinity of the plant, failure to obtain licenses, absorption by larger enterprises, and, most
important, bankruptcy. Since the late 1960s the number of
plants in actual operation has stabilized between 120 and
130.

The boom in plant construction reveals several characteristics. In the first place financing was easily

obtained for a time. Peruvian commercial banks were very
willing to loan money for the industry's expansion at high
interest rates. The boom was so promising, and the industry so simplified, that many entrepreneurs--even those
completely inexperienced in fisheries--were able to get
established, and learn with the development of the industry.

The role of Peruvian and foreign capital in the fishmeal industry has been the subject of considerable concern.
Foreign capital had considerable significance in the earliest stages of production. The early fishmeal plants
were equipped with machinery from the defunct California
sardine canneries, which had been forced to close by the
disappearance of sardines from the California coast.[14]
Middle-class Peruvian businessmen, frequently either
foreign-born or second-generation Peruvians, became entrepreneurs by purchasing this bargain equipment on credit,
usually from Peruvian banks. When the boom became very
speculative and many companies incurred too much debt, the
Peruvian financial oligarchs intervened, concentrating and
regrouping the industry.

Several writers have explored this pattern. François
Bourricaud believes that the pattern of letting others
take the initial risk and then appearing to reap the
profits is a typical characteristic of the Peruvian oligarchy.[15] Grant Hilliker refers to the absorptive effects
of the Peruvian oligarchy, pointing out the dominance
that the traditional oligarchs have over the new industry
through control of banking, insurance, and trade.[16] Aníbal
Quijano identifies the same process as a combination of
the primary export economy with the tertiary features of
trade, transportation, and finance.[17] David Chaplin substantiates the foreign origin of Peru's industrial entrepreneurs. He finds that the textile industry was founded
by "elite strangers," meaning that they were from cultures
highly respected in Peru; even though they may hold Peruvian citizenship, they are not fully Peruvian in the cultural sense.[18] This same pattern appears to be true, to a
considerable extent, of the fishmeal industry.

Both foreign and Peruvian capital continued to support the boom. Of the 26 top fishmeal-producing firms in
1971 (63 separate plants), five were U.S. firms, one was
Argentine one was Japanese, three were jointly owned by
Peruvian and foreign owners, and the remaining 16 were
Peruvian corporations. Production figures for 1971 show
that the Peruvian firms produced only slightly more than
half the meal produced by these top 26 firms.[19] The ten
firms owned by Luis Banchero Rossi, the leading producer

of the industry and a second-generation Italian, produced nearly three times as much as the second highest producer, a U.S. corporation.[20] Foreign capital, while never dominating the industry, has been significant enough to cause sensitive Peruvian nationalists to worry that foreign capitalists were once more exploiting and dissipating a valuable Peruvian natural resource without adequately protecting Peru's interests.

The fishmeal boom was also very visible in the rapid increase in fishing vessels, bolicheras. The number of these purse seiners increased over three times, and the capacity over five times, between 1959 and 1962.[21] At one time there were as many as 47 separate small boat builders constructing the seiners. Most of them were small, underfinanced operations; some worked in vacant lots and streets in their eagerness to participate in an industry that had such a low entry barrier. In 1963, however, there was widespread failure brought on by poor fishing, curtailment of bank credit, and government fears of overfishing.[22]

Peruvian fishmeal is almost entirely an export product, with the major markets being the developed nations, especially the United States and West Germany. The United States was the major consumer for a number of years early in the boom period. The more recent high prices for fishmeal apparently caused the U.S. animal feeds mixers to turn to substitute proteins, especially soya beans. The peak of U.S. imports of Peruvian fishmeal was the 544,044 metric tons imported in 1968; the decline is indicated by the 1970 figure of 155,172 metric tons for U.S. imports. In that year West Germany purchased 487,387 metric tons.[23] By 1972, however the United States was again the largest single buyer with purchases of 317,000 metric tons; West Germany was the second largest buyer with 292,000. These rapid shifts in the quantities imported by the United States were influenced by the spiraling costs of soya beans, as well as by recognition that Peru's anchovy supply was seriously depleted, at least temporarily.[24]

The rapidly developing poultry industries in Italy, Spain, and Japan are growing markets for Peru's fishmeal. In addition Peru is hopeful that the Latin American market, especially in Mexico, will also develop rapidly. Interestingly both Spain and Mexico have some restrictions on imported fishmeal in an effort to protect their own small fishmeal industries.[25]

The Peruvian economy is heavily dependent on fishmeal exports--they have accounted for about one-third of the total Peruvian export earnings in recent years. This is

usually more than the value of Peru's copper exports (see
Table 2). There are certain indirect costs involved in
the heavy dependence on the fishmeal export. First, there
is the decline in guano production for Peruvian agriculture.
In addition fishmeal production exerts a vast drain on the
available power and water supplies in Peru. Each ton of
fishmeal produced requires six to ten cubic meters of water
and 600 kwh of electricity.[26]

TABLE 2

Peruvian Exports
(percentages of total)

Product	1963	1964	1965	1966	1967	1968	1969	1970
Fish products	22.1	24.4	27.2	27.0	26.9	27.1	25.0	33.7
Copper	15.7	15.1	17.6	24.4	26.2	27.0	30.1	23.8
Cotton	16.5	13.3	12.7	11.1	7.3	7.8	7.9	5.0
Sugar	11.7	9.3	5.5	6.2	7.0	7.3	4.3	5.8
Iron ore	6.6	5.7	6.8	7.0	8.2	7.2	7.9	6.9
Lead	3.0	4.8	5.4	4.5	4.0	6.5	4.0	3.4
Silver	6.4	6.6	5.7	5.4	5.6	4.1	6.9	6.0
Zinc	2.8	5.7	5.2	4.4	4.7	3.8	4.9	5.0
Coffee	4.6	5.4	4.2	3.7	3.8	3.4	3.5	4.2
Petroleum	1.8	1.4	1.4	1.0	1.1	1.3	0.7	0.7
Other	8.8	8.3	8.3	5.3	5.2	4.5	4.8	5.5

Sources: Peruvian Times Fisheries Supplement, 1969,
p. 46; Anuario de Pesca, 1970-1971, p. 198.

The 1960 world fishmeal price suffered a drastic decline to about half of what it had been in the previous
year. Faced with this situation, the producers set about
to stabilize the market, establishing two fisheries organizations. The Sociedad Nacional de Pesqueria (SNP) is a
national trade association, which sent delegates to the
World Fishmeal Producers Congress in Paris in September
1960. This Congress produced the Paris Agreement, which
established export quotas for each country producing fishmeal, ratifying the existing trade patterns. Peru's quota
was the largest, 60 percent. Other member nations were
Angola, Iceland, Norway, South Africa, Chile, and Denmark.

In addition to the SNP a group of Peruvian producers
established the Consorcio Pesquero, a marketing cooperative,
to handle the coordinated marketing of Peruvian fishmeal.
Consorcio members sold fishmeal to the cooperative, which,
in turn, placed the commodity on the world market. Some
80 percent of the industry voluntarily joined the Consorcio
in 1966 because of fears of a quasi-nationalization by the
Peruvian government.[27] The relative effectiveness of the
Consorcio's attempts to regulate the market, stabilize
prices, and increase demand for fishmeal forestalled direct
governmental actions against the fishmeal producers. Regulations were placed on fishing, instead, in order to protect the anchovy source.

Naturally the Peruvian government has been concerned
about the fishmeal industry, as well as about the Peruvian
economy's dependence on fishmeal exports. The early governmental efforts were to encourage resource conservation
of the anchovy. The Instituto del Mar del Peru (IMARPE)
campaigned, rather ineffectively, for industrial self-
restraint until 1965, when it ordered a veda, "closed
season," for one month. In that year the natural disaster
known as El Niño struck the Peruvian coast. Oceanographic
experts explain that the abundance of anchovies is due to
the temperature of the offshore currents. Prevailing
southerly winds force the warmer surface waters out to sea,
allowing the deeper nutrient-rich Humboldt Current to surface. These rich waters feed the profusion of fish. Occasionally, however, the currents change temporarily, the
surface waters warm, and millions of anchovies and birds
starve.[28] El Niño occurred in 1965 and resulted in the
death of an estimated 15 million birds, reduced guano production to one sixth of normal,[29] and diminished fishmeal
production by 1.7 million tons from the preceding year.
After that year the fishmeal producers accepted regulation
of the industry as a necessity. Supreme Decree 005 of
January 28, 1966 established a closed season during the
spawning season from May to August. Every year since then
a veda has been declared, although they vary somewhat in
length and timing according to the scientific studies of
IMARPE.

Because they have accepted the veda as worthwhile, the
fishmeal producers like to think that they have learned to
regulate their fishing at the maximum sustainable level.
It is true, however, that the quantity of fish caught has
increased even in years when the legal fishing season was
reduced by more than half.[30] Fisheries are different from
other renewable resources in that regulation in order to

maximize physical output means the establishment of uneconomic regulations. Restrictions are usually placed on the duration of seasons, types of gear, mesh sizes, or minimum weight limit. This means that intensity of effort increases to offset losses in output, which, in turn, means continued or even accelerated stock depletion.[31]

Several scientists believe that the anchovies are not adequately protected by the veda. Georg Bergstrom estimates that the basic anchovy resource has been reduced from 25 million to 12 to 13 million tons annually. With the annual catch at approximately 10 million tons he thinks the resource would be dangerously depleted.[32] But both Garth Murphy and Milner Schaefer agree that the maximum sustainable yield is 7.5 million tons rather than 10 million tons, although their recommendations differ. Murphy suggested lengthening the veda so that more fish would be spawned.[33] Schaefer concluded that the anchovy fleet was too large and needed closer regulation.[34]

Clearly a major result of the fishmeal boom is the excess capacity of the industry. This is especially true since the government began limiting the anchovy catch.[35] The industry estimates that existing plants and fleet could catch and process the limit, approximately 10 million tons annually, in three or four months of normal working hours. The government prevents this by artificially lengthening the fishing season. In 1971, for example, there were vedas declared from January to February and from June to August; and boats were limited to only four days fishing per week. This system provides steadier work for the fishermen, but the fishmeal companies complain that it raises their costs with the more pronounced stop-go system.[36]

After 1960's temporary slump in world prices, the efforts to stabilize marketing, the worldwide quota system, and rising demand for fishmeal produced higher prices. The rise in prices, plus the volume of fishmeal being traded, attracted the world's speculators in cereal futures.[37] They began to buy, especially during 1962 and 1963, from an increasing number of independent producers. During this period another serious financial crisis occurred, caused not only by the speculation in fishmeal futures, but also by the credit squeeze in the increasing production costs.

The Peruvian fishmeal producers lack information on consumer markets, which in this period left them at a disadvantage with the buyers who had had plenty of experience in trading the other ingredients of animal feeds. Fishmeal was sold either for immediate shipment or in futures, leading naturally to speculation. The seller of futures may be selling uncaught or unborn fish, and the buyer takes "long" or "short" positions according to his studies of the market. Since the independent producers did not sell at an average price, and since they sold at a price which included costs and freight, the buyer became the actual owner of the fishmeal in port. This means that from the time the buyer acquires lots of fishmeal FOB (free on board) he is free to ship the meal to the destination offering the best current price in terms of its "long" or "short" positions. Thus there was considerable unreliability in fulfillment of contracts.

LA MARCHA HACIA EL OESTE

Peru's revolutionary junta government, which came to power in 1968, has made a number of changes in the fisheries industries.[38] In the first place a new Ministry of Fisheries was established with General Javier Tantaleán made minister. Fisheries matters had been handled previously by a section of the Agriculture Ministry. The new ministry demonstrates the junta's determination to handle fisheries matters more authoritatively. The policies of the new ministry have been labelled La Marcha Hacia el Oeste, which means "The March to the West." This symbolic slogan represents the government's determination to improve the life of the traditional fishermen, to improve national nutrition, and to continue the harvest in the full 200-mile claim area of Peru's territorial waters without increasing dependence on anchovy fishmeal.

The second step that the junta took in dealing with fisheries reforms was to nationalize the marketing of fishmeal. In April 1970 the National Fishmeal and Fishoil Marketing Corporation (EPCHAP) was established by Decree Law 18212, which forbade the unauthorized sales of fishmeal. This decree caused fishmeal futures to rise $5 in New York and $18 in Hamburg. As with other junta regulatory activities the move had been telegraphed to the industry well in advance of its issuance. Both the industry and the foreign buyers had been expecting the ban, and had agreed to the export of about 750,000 tons prior to the decree.[39]

EPCHAP replaced the Consorcio and the three other independent marketing channels, intending to carry out all sales in a planned and coordinated manner so as to avoid wild fluctuations in fishmeal prices, as well as guaranteeing predictable delivery and contract fulfillments to the

consumers. The major reform is a procedural one--all contracts are made on a C & F (cost and freight) or a CIF
(cost, insurance, and freight) basis, with EPCHAP signing
for shipping and delivery. This move to eliminate the
middleman means that speculation in fishmeal contracts has
been virtually eliminated; now the buyers are frequently
the animal feeds mixers themselves.[40] It must be pointed
out, however, that the increasing sales to Eastern European
nations sometimes result in trade patterns similar to those
of the international speculators in the past. The state
organizations that buy for the Eastern European nations
sometimes find it to their advantage to make bilateral
deals with buyers in Western Europe, selling their tonnage
to them.

EPCHAP's record in 1971 created what the SNP warned
was a very grave crisis for the industry. When EPCHAP
began its operations in June 1970, prices were high and
meal was plentiful. Soon, however, EPCHAP began reserving
fishmeal, and held out for higher prices for ten months,
during what was actually a falling market. More than one
million tons of fishmeal accumulated on Peruvian docks in
early 1971. EPCHAP removed the speculative middlemen in
New York, Hamburg, and London, only to take over fishmeal
speculating on behalf of the Peruvian nation.[41] In order
to keep the price up, EPCHAP reported a 10-million-ton
anchovy catch when actually there had been twelve million
tons caught.[42]

There are three main goals of the General Fisheries
Law: (1) development of a table fish industry; (2) improvement of the efficiency of the fishmeal industry and
encouragement of the transfer of control of foreign-owned
fishmeal companies to Peruvian hands; and (3) redistribution of income among fishermen and plant employees. To
achieve these goals the law established three types of
priority in fisheries. The first priority is food, or
table, fish; the second priority is non-food fishing (seal-
ing, pearling, etc.) and the third priority is fishing for
indirect human consumption (fishmeal).

The third and major action of the revolutionary government in regard to fisheries was the General Fisheries
Law of March 25, 1971, Decree Law No. 18810, which is designed to change the shape of Peruvian fisheries in accordance with the government's plans to change the economic
and social structures of the nation. Quijano points out
that the main features of the law were being discussed
knowledgeably by the industry for months before the decree
was made public. In fact it seems apparent that the

General Fisheries Law was drawn up in rather close coordi-
nation with the industry. Fisheries Minister Javier
Tantaleán, for example, had toured the nation's major 'ports
with Banchero Rossi and had asked him to help organize the
table fishing industry.[43]

Currently the table fish industry--priority one--is
the recipient of the junta's greatest interest. The development of a table fish industry is to be achieved with government loans as well as with tax incentives, both to new
fishing cooperatives formed by artisanal fishermen and to
companies involved in food fishing on a larger scale. A
number of incentives are granted to companies to increase
their production. Fishmeal companies are allowed to make
tax-free reinvestments in food fishing of 100 percent of
profits. Capital goods required for food fishing can be
imported at 10 percent of normal duties and other inputs
can be imported at 20 percent of normal duties providing
that equivalent local products are not available. Those
who have had nothing to do with the fishmeal industry may
invest up to 50 percent of their net income, free of income taxes, in food fishing enterprises. Other incentives
for first-priority companies include favorable interest
rates for loans from government development banks. In addition food fishing companies can get technical and administrative assistance from the state, although preference
for these services is given to the cooperatives of artisanal fishermen.

The question of reducing foreign ownership and control
of fishmeal companies is rather complicated. In the original law companies with more than 50 percent of stock in
foreign hands were to contract with the government by
January 1, 1972, detailing their plans for transferring
control to domestic owners. Decree Law No. 18999 (of
October 20, 1971) has superseded the General Fisheries Law
on this point, however. Foreign-controlled fishmeal companies, in accordance with the Andean Pact, are given
three years to transfer 15% of their foreign capital to
Peruvians and a maximum of 15 years to transfer 51 percent
ownership to Peruvians. Some foreign-owned companies apparently considered mergers with Peruvian companies in
order to meet these requirements.

To reduce foreign capital in the fishmeal industry,
the shareholders may sell their stock to the Comunidad
Pesquero, "fishing community," which can pay for it with
the 12 percent that the company's net income required to
be set aside each year. The fishing communities are designed to promote social solidarity between the workers,

the management, and the state. Membership in a fishing
community automatically includes all those working for a
company full time, except those who already own shares in
the company. The fishing community is run by a general
assembly of all members and by an executive body, the community council, which has the right to examine the company's books to determine the composition of the declared
profits. Union leaders are restricted from serving on the
community council.

In addition the Comunidad de Compensación Pesquera,
"fisheries compensation community," distributes shares of
the company's profits on an equal basis to all members of
the fishing community. Every year each company must de-
duct 22 percent from profits. Twelve percent of that
amount forms the fishing community's capital ownership in
the company, 8 percent goes to the community members in
cash, and the remaining 2 percent is used for a research
and training fund. The fisheries compensation community
distributes its 8 percent in two ways--half goes to each
member on an equal per capita basis and the other half is
divided on the basis of wages paid to the workers.

The 12 percent owned by the fishing community is re-
invested in the company. Currently the government plans
for it to be capitalized immediately until the fishing
community owns half the company's total capital. If the
government later decides that increased capitalization is
unwise, the community's capital will be used to buy existing stock. The fishing community is required to be represented on the company's board of directors. By the time
the community owns half the company it should also have
half the directors.[44]

In accordance with the junta's efforts to "rationalize" the fishmeal industry by improving its efficiency, a
number of orders have been decreed. In 1971 the average
production ratio for the entire fishmeal industry was 5.4
tons of anchovies to one ton of meal. The government
hoped to bring that ratio down to 5.1 to 1 by 1973. Already the most efficient companies are able to produce one
ton of meal for 4.5 or 4.4 tons of anchovies.[45] One of
the ways in which these companies have increased their
productivity is by installing stickwater plants--plants
which reprocess the liquids discarded in normal processing.
Between 15 to 20 percent more meal can be produced by
turning this waste into protein. Consequently the junta
made stickwater plants obligatory, and gave the companies
until the start of the 1972 fishing season to install them.
Moreover since 1971 fully assembled stickwater plants

cannot be imported, although component parts can be imported at greatly reduced tariffs. Stickwater plants are quite expensive, costing about $250,000 each. A complication, however, is that credit to buy stickwater plants, even from official banks, has been rather difficult to obtain. Lenders are wary, in view of the narrowing profit margins, of getting guaranteed repayment promptly.[46]

Actually more than stickwater plants is needed to make the production ratio as efficient as it is in some other countries that produce fishmeal. Most Peruvian plants should be redesigned in order to get the maximum from every step of production. A wide variety of faults plague Peruvian production including overcooking, undercooking, inadequate pressing, overloading presses, inefficient dryers, and poorly preserved fish.[47]

Since the government is now responsible for shipping fishmeal on a cost and freight basis, efforts are being made to reduce freight costs. One way of doing this is to convert from shipping meal in bags to bulk shipments, preferably in pellets. Bulk shipments eliminate the cost of the bags--about $7 per ton--and also increase the quantity of meal shipped per vessel by about 25 percent.[48] The government has also embarked on a program of expanding the infrastructures, especially deep-water port facilities, in order to speed loading time by the use of conveyor belts connected to the freighter.

In addition the government has also taken recent steps to upgrade the quality of fishmeal, especially in terms of quality certification for a more standardized product. It has also begun careful studies of the world market--the poultry and pork industries in importing countries, as well as the production of competitive proteins. All of these efforts are embodied in La Marcha Hacia el Oeste.

The government's development plan for the fishing industry for 1971-75 is based on an annual anchovy catch of 9.5 million tons and food fish catches of 600,000 tons by 1975. This will require an investment of $434 million over the five-year period, with more than half that amount, $264 million, expected from private sources and the remaining $170 million from government funds. Specific projects for these moneys include stickwater plant acquisitions, relocation and reconstruction of 15 plants that were damaged severely by the May 1970 earthquake, purchase of a food fishing fleet, and installation of technical equipment, including equipment for gas treating, fish pumping, and drainage.[49]

Naturally the sort of high payoff that was characteristic of the fishmeal boom cannot be true of table fish.

For that reason the government has proceeded vigorously to promote these developments itself, either through direct loans or tax incentives. The government has begun an ambitious program for building port facilities, constructing boats for food fishing, establishing refrigerated distribution facilities, and researching the resources and the market potential. The U.N. Food and Agriculture Organization (FAO) and Peru have a joint five-year fisheries research project, with each contributing $1 million to finance it. A primary goal is to improve Peruvian nutrition by encouraging more consumption of fish, as well as reducing the costly importation of beef and other food products. In terms of the latter goal the minister of fisheries, General Tantaleán, proposed that there should be ten meatless days every month. A decree of April 1, 1972, however, ordered 15 meatless days every month.[50]

Although the program to encourage food fishing is still quite new, it does show signs of considerable progress. The Public Fisheries Services Company (EPSEP) is responsible for implementing the program.[51] It has established ten stationary fish marketing centers around Lima as well as a number of mobile sales trailers and kiosks for the sale of fresh fish in Lima--150 kiosks were planned for completion by the end of 1972. Lima also has a new wholesale fish market in operation. There are three new fishing terminals in operation at Callao, San Jose, and Pacasmay. EPSEP has also established three inland fish centers for the distribution of fresh and frozen fish in Tacna, Arequipa, and Ayacucho; nine others are to be completed in 1972. Fresh fish is flown to the inland centers. In addition frozen fish is being stockpiled by EPSEP. These activities are accompanied by an extensive public relations campaign encouraging more fish consumption.

EPSEP's aim is to eventually create a high seas fleet to catch and process 600,000 tons per year of high-quality fish, both for domestic consumption and for export. Peru hopes eventually to export large blocks of frozen hake, merluza, to Europe and perhaps to the United States. Canneries have also increased their output, mainly tuna and bonito. There are now 23 canneries; there were 14 in 1970 and only 10 in 1969. Some canned fish is consumed domestically, but exports are rising. In 1969, 2,753 tons of canned fish were exported and in 1970, 3,464 tons were exported, primarily to Western Europe.[52]

The area of boat building has been hurt by the General Fisheries Law's limitations on expansion of the bolichera fleet. In 1971 the government decreed that for every 1.5

tons of new bolichera capacity, one ton would have to be
withdrawn. Licenses that had not been used for the previous two seasons were revoked. These limitations probably served merely to speed the natural economic cutbacks
that the boat builders would have been forced to make
eventually. Unfortunately the move toward a food fishing
industry will not offer an equivalent stimulus, although
the new fishing cooperatives have begun to place orders
for some vessels.[53] While it seems logical for the re-
dundant bolicheras to go into food fishing, and even though
some of the artisanal fishermen are being encouraged to
use bolicheras, the standard anchovy bolichera is not
equipped with refrigeration and other equipment necessary
for efficient food fishing.

FISHING CRISIS--1972-73

In 1972, in the worst shortage of anchovies in the
history of Peru's fishmeal industry, the government had to
halt all fishmeal and fishoil exports on October 1, 1972.
The junta made attempts to persuade the buyers to accept
postponements of deliveries in order to avoid the penalty
clauses in the sales contracts. The industry was devas-
tated by the lack of fish--nearly 30,000 people were reportedly out of work because of El Niño. The crisis was
so severe in fact that the fisheries minister travelled to
the United States seeking official help in understanding
the currents and periodic shortages of fish off the Peruvian coast. The United States, however, refused such
assistance until Peru would sign a bilateral agreement
allowing California tuna boats to fish unmolested in the
Peruvian claim area.[54]
After an eight-month suspension in the 1972-73 period,
fishing was resumed in March 1973. Within a few weeks,
however, it was clear that the stock was still depleted
and that many of the anchovies available were undersized.
The FAO warned that continued fishing would endanger the
very survival of anchovies in the Humboldt Current. Unofficial estimates placed the stock at some four million
tons--about one-fifth of "normal."[55]
On May 7, 1973, the Peruvian junta attempted to deal
with the fishing crisis by nationalizing the entire fishmeal industry. A package of legislative decrees nationalized the industry and established a new company, Pesca
Peru, to run the industry. In many ways nationalization
was merely the final step in increased government controls

of this all-important industry. The junta already controlled marketing of fishmeal, testing of fishmeal, equipment requirements for fishmeal plants, and financing of the
industry in state banks. It was the latter feature that no
doubt triggered the expropriation. The fishmeal industry
has always required large-scale financing; this was even
more true during the 1972-73 crisis. The result was that
the industry was heavily mortgaged to the government itself. The fisheries minister put the total industrial
debt at about double the "net worth" of the industry. Besides the high debt level another reason stipulated by the
government was the need to "rationalize" the industry by
reducing overcapacity of the fleet and plants.

At the time of nationalization the industry consisted
of nearly 50 companies that had about 97 plants in operation. The fleet consisted of some 1,400 boats. There
were about 27,000 people employed in the industry. The
government claimed that about 37 percent of the industry
was foreign-owned. Industry spokesmen estimated that the
total worth of the expropriated industry was about $500
million.[56] At this writing it is too early to evaluate
the nationalized fishing industry. It is also too soon to
tell if the anchovies will return in the quantities that
formerly abounded. What is clear is the enormous dependency of the entire Peruvian economy on a stable, healthy
fishmeal industry.

PERUVIAN FISHERIES AND ECONOMIC DEVELOPMENT

In assessing the role of fisheries in economic development there is not a great deal of historical precedent
to examine. Harold Innis investigated this role in his
economic history of the cod fisheries in the Maritime
Provinces and New England. During the mercantile era,
which concentrated on exporting staples to developed areas,
fishing stimulated shipping, trade, vigorous commercial
organizations, and population growth. As industrial capitalism replaced mercantile trade the impact of fisheries
was less salutary. The regions had limited agricultural
development, a lag in governmental development, and a dependence on an export product that bound the regions, especially Newfoundland, to the revenues produced by fisheries. As Innis points out, "An industry which flourished
with commercialism and an international economy was crushed
by the demands of capitalism and nationalism."[57]
Despite the lack of historical studies, there have
been several recent studies of staple exports as a stimulus

for development rather than a hindrance. These writers are
no doubt reacting against the "trade pessimists" who have
dominated a great deal of the economic development theory
of the postwar period. The "trade pessimists," such as
Ragnar Nurkse and Raúl Prebisch, maintain that an export
economy hinders economic development because the terms of
trade for the producers of raw materials and primary products are deteriorating. In Latin America, in particular,
Prebisch's center-periphery theory of the world economy has
been popular. According to this theory the exchange of
primary goods for manufactured goods victimized the developing countries in a new form of economic colonialism.
The "trade pessimists" generally advocate one or more of
four alternatives for development: import substitution
industrialization (ISI), commodity agreements, trade pref-
erences, and regional trade associations. A study by
Magali Larson and Arlene Bergman focuses similar criticism
on the Peruvian economy. They believe that Peru's export
economy fosters a double dependence--the external dependence on the market and an internal colonialism for those
who do not have access to the benefits of the export-
oriented economy. They also believe that the recent tremendous growth of the Peruvian economy has been achieved
at the price of even greater concentration of income.[58]
The "trade optimists" believe that trade has been an effective vehicle of growth recently for some nations, such
as Japan, Taiwan and Israel. They believe the same could
be true of some other countries with other exports, providing the less developed country itself removes obstacles
that it has placed in the way of exports of primary products.[59]

Charles Gibson believes that trade has not stimulated
Ecuadorian growth largely because Ecuador has not allowed
it to do so. He says that restrictions on foreign trade,
encouragement of ISI, neglect of agriculture, and the lack
of internal reforms prevented Ecuador from building both a
healthier international trade and an internal market as
well. He concludes that the Ecuadorians in power--the
politicians, large landowners, and businessmen--benefit
from the stagnant economic system.[60]

Joseph Grunwald and Philip Musgrove, while not dis-
agreeing with the "trade pessimist" school, believe that
the Latin American emphasis on improving the terms of trade
is not the panacea it has been assumed to be. Export
earnings can contribute to economic development, especially
by providing the income to pay for imported food products
and components for the ISI. They maintain that if industrialization continues to be emphasized, exports of Latin

America's natural resources must increase in order to pay for the imports required for industrial expansion. Therefore exports must play a "major supporting role" in development.[61]

The most important work by a "trade optimist" for our study is Roemer's full-length study of the Peruvian fishmeal industry as an example of a successful export-led developing economy. He believes that Peru has successfully promoted diversification and industrialization because of its exports, with the export income providing foreign exchange that was invested in development expenditures. Most natural resource exploitations have had very weak linkages to the rest of the economy, but Roemer finds that this was not so of fishmeal because it stimulated the production of goods manufactured in Peru. Fishmeal was responsible directly for the development of four new industries in Peru: boat construction, net production, manufacture of processing equipment, and the manufacture of jute sacks. Furthermore the fishmeal boom was an important stimulus to such other industries as paper, petroleum, insurance, transportation, storage, power, and financial institutions.[62] While the fishmeal industry was not able to stimulate inland industries, with the exception of the jute farmers in the jungle, it did spread along the length of the 1,400-mile coast, thus reducing, to a degree, the economic concentration in Lima and Callao. Chimbote, in fact, became a major center for the fishmeal industry. Roemer concludes that the fishmeal industry was not an enclave economy, with almost two-thirds of fishmeal's foreign exchange earnings being retained in Peru.[63]

Anthony Scott has suggested that the "common property" nature of fisheries and the resultant wasteful competition prevent most fisheries from playing a very significant role in economic development. The fisheries to which he refers are very different, however, from the unique Peruvian anchovy fishery. He adds that there are three possible ways in which fisheries can contribute to national development: by increasing food supplies, by providing a source of export income, and by stimulating related industries.[64] It seems obvious that Peruvian fishmeal has already successfully accomplished the latter two; La Marcha Hacia el Oeste gives further impressive evidence that it will be able to accomplish the former, as well as increase the quantities of table fish for export. Undoubtedly the domestic market for fishmeal will grow as the Peruvian poultry and livestock farms expand. It is also possible that research on the refined version of fishmeal, fish protein concentrate (FPC) or fishflour, will make it more palatable for direct human consumption and thus more appealing for the Peruvian diet. None of these stimuli for better nutrition and wider variety in the national diet would have been likely without the development of the export fishery.[65]

One other contribution that fisheries make to the Peruvian economy is in providing employment. Although the number of those employed in the fishing industry is not really large--around 30,000--it is regarded as a beneficial source of employment. It is true that much of the employment offered by fisheries in developing countries manifests basic unemployment, a lack of alternative employment, and the common-property nature of fisheries.[66] In Peru, even though the fishmeal industry is not too demanding technologically, it has raised the level of skills of its employees. Fishermen and supervisors are trained by the unions and companies in order to reduce accidents, to increase the catch, and to make the industry more efficient. Some 9,000 laborers have been trained in such subjects and skills as workshop mathematics, welding, mechanical and electrical maintenance, and operation and maintenance of diesel engines and boilers. Supervisors have studied human relations and improvement of working methods. Beyond this immediate level Peru has also increased the level of its knowledge and expertise in marine resources through IMARPE and predecessor organizations, with the support of both the U.N. and the fishmeal industry. Oceanography is taught in several Peruvian universities.[67]

What conclusions can be reached about the role of fisheries in the Peruvian economy? As a source of government income that is channeled to development expenditures, and as a provider of consequential employment along the Peruvian coast, the fishmeal industry makes important contributions to development. In addition there is evidence of a number of rewarding linkages to the rest of the Peruvian economy; and they are apparently going to include forward as well as backward linkages. Furthermore even though there are similarities between the guano and fishmeal booms, fishmeal is not repeating the performance of the guano enclave. One of the primary reasons for this is that the administrative skills and knowledge, as well as the understanding of the economic implications, of Peruvian officials are far higher than they were during the guano boom. These intentions were evident in the prejunta governments; it is even more true of the Velasco government's efforts to control the pitfalls of the export-dependent economy. It should be noted, however, that certain aspects of the externality of fishmeal exports have had crucial political effects in terms of influencing or dominating governmental decisions relating to devaluation and balance of payments.

Carlos Astiz believes that the fishmeal industry, like guano in the nineteenth century, provided a stimulus for the traditional coastal upper class that was necessary for its continued dominance of Peru's social and economic patterns. The episode which substantiates this belief was the campaign waged by the fishmeal producers, as leading spokesmen of other export interests, and the financial institutions closely involved with the fishmeal expansion, for the 1967 devaluation of the sol.[68] The sol had been stationary at 27 to the dollar for many years, but as Peruvian inflation increased, the purchasing power of the dollar was reduced. This meant that those engaged in the export economy--the traditional coastal oligarchs engaged in cotton and sugar production as well as the new fishmeal industrialists and foreign investors--found that their export economy was less rewarding, while the importation of other goods was relatively less expensive. The Peruvian balance of payments was maintained favorably throughout the early 1960s at the expense of the exporters, who stood to gain from devaluation because they could get more sols for the dollars they gained abroad.

The exporters mounted their attack on the sol in early 1967. Fishmeal shipments were delayed, exporters hoarded their dollars, and demand for dollars mounted as the rumors of forthcoming devaluation circulated. The Central Reserve Bank used dollar reserves to maintain the exchange rate, reportedly draining its dollar reserves to $60 million.[69] At that point the fishmeal producers began pressuring President Belaunde Terry and the Congress either for elimination of export taxes or devaluation. The Sociedad Nacional de Pesquera sent a 100-member delegation to lobby in Congress, widely publicizing their demands in the nation's press.[70] The former demand, elimination of export taxes, would have created a large deficit, thus sabotaging Belaunde's plans for development projects. When the fishmeal producers failed to receive immediate satisfaction, they threatened to increase the pressures with the support of other exporters and banking allies.

The crisis was precipitated by the political struggle over the 1967 budget. Congress balked at adopting any new taxes to finance the development projects that Belaunde proposed. The traditional upper class wanted these projects curtailed anyway, because such programs as agrarian reform, rural communal development, increased educational spending, and road construction were directly threatening to the status quo. Belaunde's position was one of trying to avoid devaluation by agreeing to some reduction of development spending in return for some tax increases; he refused, however, to cut the budget as much as was demanded. Therefore, in order to protect some limited agrarian reform and public works expenditures, the president ordered that the Central Reserve Bank stop supporting the sol, which dropped to 43 to the dollar. Astiz concludes that the devaluation was motivated politically in order to reverse whatever income redistribution was taking place as a result of the stable balance of payments and the modest development projects, and that it also provided the traditional upper-class exporters with approximately 63 percent more sols for their export-earned dollars.[71]

With the close interrelationship between politics and economics in Peru, it is not surprising that the fishmeal industry sought and achieved a political solution to its economic problems. The details of this story of political pressure leave little doubt as to why the revolutionary government took such early steps to regulate the fishmeal producers. It does, however, raise anew the question of the role of the fishmeal industry in promoting Peruvian development. The devaluation meant that those involved in other industrialization had to pay more for imported equipment and raw materials. It also meant that the cost of living for the ordinary Peruvian citizen jumped appreciably while wages failed to maintain the same rate of increase. Fishmeal has been very beneficial in promoting development on some scores: stimulating linked industries and providing foreign exchange for development projects. But the development stimulated by fishmeal has not been achieved without some very crucial social, political, and economic costs being exacted from the entire nation.

NOTES

1. Eric R. Wolf and Edward C. Hansen, The Human Condition in Latin America (New York: Oxford University Press, 1972), pp. 3-13; Joseph Grunwald and Philip Musgrove, Natural Resources in Latin American Development (Baltimore: Johns Hopkins Press, 1970), chap. 1.

2. Frederick B. Pike, The Modern History of Peru (New York: Frederick A. Praeger, Inc., 1967), pp. 91-98.

3. Watt Stewart, <u>Chinese Bondage in Peru: A History of the Chinese Coolie in Peru, 1849-1874</u> (Durham, N.C.: Duke University Press, 1951).

4. Jonathan Levin, <u>The Export Economies: Their Pattern of Development in Historical Perspective</u> (Cambridge, Mass.: Harvard University Press, 1960), pp. 113-14.

5. Pike, op. cit., p. 97.

6. James L. Payne, <u>Labor and Politics in Peru: The System of Political Bargaining</u> (New Haven, Conn.: Yale University Press, 1965), pp. 30-31.

7. William J. Mills, "Peru's Fishmeal Industry," U.S. Department of Agriculture, Foreign Agriculture Service, FAS M-204 (April 1969), pp. 3-4.

8. Wilbert McLeod Chapman, "Perspectiva de la pesqueria en el mundo," <u>Primer Seminario Latinoamericano sobre el Oceano Pacifico Oriental</u> (Lima: Universidad Nacional Mayor de San Marcos, 1966), p. 29.

9. Georg Borgstrom, "Are the Oceans a Reserve of the Well-Fed World?" All-University Lecture, Yale University, New Haven, Conn., November 24, 1968; Georg Borgstrom, "The Japanese-Soviet Challenge to World Fisheries," <u>Proceedings of the Gulf and Caribbean Fisheries Institute</u>, 17th Annual Session, November 1964, pp. 3-7.

10. Foreign Area Studies Division, American University, <u>Area Handbook for Peru</u> (Washington: U.S. Army, 1965), p. 585.

11. Peggy Massey, "Is Fishmeal a Threat to Peru's Guano Birds?" <u>Peruvian Times Fisheries Supplement 1972</u>, pp. 37-39.

12. Clements R. Markham, <u>A History of Peru</u> (London: Charles H. Sergel & Company, 1892), pp. 343-486.

13. Michael Roemer, <u>Fishing for Growth: Export-Led Development in Peru, 1950-1967</u> (Cambridge, Mass.: Harvard University Press, 1970), pp. 81-83.

14. Wilbert McLeod Chapman, "Industry and the Economy of the Sea," <u>Governor's Conference on California and the World Ocean</u> (Los Angeles: California Museum of Science and Industry, 1964), pp. 53-55.

15. François Bourricaud, <u>Power and Society in Contemporary Peru</u> (New York: Praeger Publishers, 1970), p. 46. This work was originally published in French in 1967. See also Magali Sarfatti Larson and Arlene Eisen Bergman, <u>Social Stratification in Peru</u> (Berkeley, Calif.: Institute of International Studies, University of California, 1969), p. 268. The impression that the earliest entrepreneurs were immigrants to Peru or their descendants is reinforced by the brief biographical sketches of

important industry leaders in the <u>Peruvian Times Fisheries Supplement 1969</u>.

16. Grant Hilliker, <u>The Politics of Reform in Peru: The Aprista and Other Mass Parties of Latin America</u> (Baltimore: Johns Hopkins Press, 1971), p. 38.

17. Anibal Quijano Obregon, "Tendencies in Peruvian Development and in the Class Structure," in James Petras and Maurice Zeitlin, eds., <u>Latin America: Reform or Revolution</u> (New York: Fawcett Publications, Inc., 1968), pp. 292-308, 322.

18. David Chaplin, <u>The Peruvian Industrial Labor Force</u> (Princeton, N.J.: Princeton University Press, 1967), pp. 34, 100.

19. "The Top Fish Meal Producers," <u>Peruvian Times Fisheries Supplement 1972</u>, p. 68.

20. Banchero, the son of an Italian grocer, achieved a rags-to-riches biography in his early entry into the fishmeal boom. His management firm, OYSSA, owns eight of the nation's most efficient fishmeal plants, several boatyards including the nation's largest, a fishoil refinery, and a table fish enterprise. Outside the maritime industries, the Banchero empire also owns food canneries, six daily newspapers, and interests in mining, shipping, banking, and insurance. Banchero was murdered on January 1, 1972, apparently by his gardener's son. Despite the murderer's alleged confession, speculation about the bizarre nature of the murder, fed by the colorful career and wealth of Banchero, received much attention in the Peruvian press. See "Luis Banchero and the Oyssa Empire," <u>Peruvian Fisheries Supplement 1972</u>, p. 26; <u>Latin America</u> 6, no. 11, March 17, 1972.

21 G. Saetoredal, I. Tsukayama, and B. Alegre, "Fluctuaciones en la abundancia del stock de anchoveta en 1959-1962," <u>Instituto del Mar del Peru Boletin</u> 1, no. 2 (1965): 91.

22. Roemer, op. cit., pp. 86-87.

23. <u>Anuario de Pesca, 1970-1971</u>, pp. 144-45, 200-05.

24. <u>Peruvian Times</u>, July 27, 1973, p. 2.

25. Alfredo Granda, "The Marketing of Fishmeal," <u>Peruvian Times Fisheries Supplement 1970</u>, pp. 30-31.

26. Grunwald and Musgrove, op. cit., p. 476.

27. New York <u>Times</u>, November 21, 1966, p. 75.

28. Robert C. Cowen, <u>Frontiers of the Sea: The Story of Oceanographic Exploration</u> (Garden City: Doubleday, 1960), p. 164. The name <u>El Niño</u>, the child, is explained in folklore because the pattern of ecological imbalance arrives every seven or eight years with the Christmas season.

29. New York _Times_, March 13, 1966, p. 24.
30. _Anuario de Pesca, 1967-1968_, p. 95.
31. Francis T. Christy, Jr. and Anthony Scott, _The Common Wealth in Ocean Fisheries: Some Problems of Growth and Economic Allocation_ (Baltimore: Johns Hopkins Press, 1965), pp. 222-23; Donald E. Bevan, "Methods of Fishery Regulation," in _The Fisheries: Problems in Resource Management_, ed. James A. Crutchfield (Seattle: University of Washington Press, 1965), pp. 38-39; Expert Meeting on the Economic Effects of Fishery Regulation, Ottawa, 1961, _Economic Effects of Fishery Regulation_ (working paper), ed. R. Hamlisch (Rome: FAO, 1962).
32. Georg Borgstrom, quoted by Robert Cahn, "Making Economic Aid Effective," _Current_ 104 (February 1969): 42.
33. Garth I. Murphy, "Menos de 7,500,000 T. M. rendimiento sostenible de la anchoveta," _Anuario de Pesca, 1967-1968_, pp. 56-59.
34. Milner B. Schaefer, "Para análisis de dinámica pesquera es basica la marcacion de anchoveta," _Anuario de Pesca, 1967-1968_, pp. 72-77.
35. Roemer, op. cit., p. 88.
36. Nicholas Asheshov, "Government Takes Strong Position on Peru's Fishing Development," _Peruvian Times Fisheries Supplement 1972_, p. 21.
37. Granda, op. cit., p. 29.
38. Medidas y recomendaciones para la reforma del complejo pesquero," _Anuario de Pesca_, 1968-1969, pp. 14-24.
39. _Wall Street Journal_, April 21, 1970, p. 26.
40. Granda, op. cit., pp. 30-31.
41. "EPCHAP Settling Down After Uneven Start," _Peruvian Times Fisheries Supplement 1972_, pp. 23-25.
42. Los Angeles _Times_, August 14, 1972, Sec. I.
43. Anibal Quijano, _Nationalism and Capitalism in Peru: A Study in Neo-Imperialism_ (New York: Monthly Review Press, 1971), p. 29.
44. "Tax Incentives and Worker Participation in the Fishing Industry," _Peruvian Times Fisheries Supplement 1972_, pp. 56-57.
45. Asheshov, op. cit., p. 21; "La ley general de pesqueria: hacia una sociedad mas justa en el Peru," _Anuario de Pesca, 1970-1971_, pp. 126-34.
46. "Stickwater Plants Being Installed," _Peruvian Times Fisheries Supplement 1972_, p. 47 and "Stickwater Plants--Turning Leftovers into Money," _Peruvian Times Fisheries Supplement 1970_, p. 25.
47. Doreen Gillespie, "More Meal Wanted for Every Ton of Anchovy," _Peruvian Times Fisheries Supplement 1972_, p. 55.

48. Mills, op. cit., p. 5. Unfortunately bulk shipments will weaken the jute industry, which Roemer found to be the one instance of the fishmeal industry directly stimulating inland development.

49. "The Government's Plans for the Fishing Industry," Peruvian Times Fisheries Supplement 1972, pp. 42-43.

50. Latin America 6, no. 9 (March 3, 1972).

51. Luis Villacorta Boydo, "La EPSEP y la nueva orientación de la pesca para consuma humano," Anuario de Pesca, 1970-1971, pp. 162-65.

52. "Fish Canning on the Way Up," Peruvian Times Fisheries Supplement 1972, p. 33.

53. "Boat Builders Take a Closer Look at Food Fish," Peruvian Times Fisheries Supplement 1972, p. 46.

54. Latin America 6, no. 38, September 15, 1972.

55. Peruvian Times, April 20, 1973, p. 4.

56. Peruvian Times, May 11, 1973, p. 1.

57. Harold A. Innis, The Cod Fisheries: The History of an International Economy, rev. ed. (Toronto: University of Toronto Press, 1954), p. 497.

58. Larson and Bergman, op. cit., pp. 290-93.

59. Charles R. Gibson, Foreign Trade in the Economic Development of Small Nations: The Case of Ecuador (New York: Praeger Publishers, 1971), pp. 5-10; Roemer, op. cit., pp. 2-31. Both Gibson and Roemer differentiate between the "trade pessimists" and the "trade optimists." See also William P. Glade and Jon G. Udell, "The Marketing Concept and Economic Development: Peru," Journal of Inter-American Studies 10, no. 4 (October 1968): 533-46.

60. Gibson, op. cit., p. 264.

61. Grunwald and Musgrove, op. cit., p. 34.

62. Roemer, op. cit., pp. 108-21.

63. Ibid., p. 167.

64. Anthony D. Scott, "Fisheries Development and National Economic Development," Proceedings of the International Conference on Tropical Oceanography, Nov. 17-21, 1965 (Miami: University of Miami Press, 1967), pp. 334-45 (hereafter cited as Tropical Oceanography).

65. Chapman, "Perspectiva de la pesqueria en el mundo," op. cit., pp. 29-30.

66. James A. Storer, "Aspects of Fisheries in the Developing Philippines Economy," Tropical Oceanography, p. 367.

67. Alfredo Freyre, "Fishery Development in Peru," Tropical Oceanography, pp. 406-08.

68. Carlos Alberto Astiz, Pressure Groups and Power Elites in Peruvian Politics (Ithaca, N.Y.: Cornell University Press, 1969), pp. 118-22.

69. Bobbie B. Smetherman and Robert M. Smetherman, "Fishmeal and the Peruvian Economy," The Quarterly Review of Economics and Business 10, no. 3 (Autumn 1970):   43.

70. Astiz, op. cit., p. 192.

71. Ibid., pp. 121-22.

5

THE U.S. TUNA INDUSTRY: DOMESTIC PRESSURE AND INTERNATIONAL PENETRATION

The U.S. tuna industry is a complex industry with many rapidly changing variables. Furthermore, within the broader realm of the U.S. fishing industry, there is growing fragmentation over the width of national fishery zones according to the species fished. It is also obvious that these variables have had considerable, and complicated, impacts on inter-American and international relations. The variety of problems dealing with tunas point to them as an international resource and to their conservation as an international problem. Recognition of this characteristic has been slow in reaching international organizations. It was not until the FAO meeting on tuna in 1962 that there was any organized international recognition of the international aspects of tuna: stock migration, interocean fishing efforts, and international trade.[1]

Paradoxically the U.S. tuna industry has been both early and late in recognizing the international ramifications of the tuna resource. Naturally because of the seizures, the U.S. tuna industry became aware very early of the international problems of tuna "ownership." The reaction of the U.S. tuna industry to this recognition was to put considerable domestic pressure on the U.S. government to apply concerted, sometimes retaliatory, pressures on other governments. In fact this pattern continues to be the industry's primary political tactic, even though it is obviously unsuccessful.

ECONOMIC CHARACTERISTICS OF THE TUNA INDUSTRY

Financially U.S. tuna fishing is a gamble. The industry faces a variety of risks that include poor catches, overfishing, seizures or other harassment by other nations, and concerns such as the recent scare over the mercury content of fish. The industry also is concerned about attempts to prohibit the inadvertent killing of porpoises by the purse-seining technique of catching tuna. A major worry of the industry is that of increased international competition for the resources from heavily subsidized foreign fishing fleets. These prospects not only intensify the dangers of overfishing, but they also warrant concern about increased national claims to ownership of the resource.

Despite the risks involved in tuna fishing, it is clear that the gamble is often a very remunerative one for many in the industry. World demand for tuna, already very high, is increasing even though the supply is relatively fixed. This means that the prices are high, attracting even more entrants into the industry. Currently there are some 123 U.S. tuna clippers of 100 tons of frozen tuna capacity operating from U.S. ports. The value of these vessels represents an investment conservatively estimated at above $160 million.[2] The 1970 wholesale value of canned tuna was about $383 million, or slightly more than $500 million in retail value. In addition the industry processed about $3.9 million in meal and oil as well as a significant part of the $105.2 million wholesale value derived from fish-based animal foods.[3] In 1973 the canneries agreed to pay $477 per ton for yellowfin--an increase of $65 in two years--and $447 per ton for skipjack.[4] Perhaps one of the reasons the role of the U.S. tuna industry as a penetrator in Latin American politics is so inflammatory is that the penetration is so lucrative.

Approximately 80 percent of the U.S. tuna fishermen are Portuguese-Americans. The nucleus of these fishing families was established in California as early as 1912, with others arriving after World War I. Many had been fishermen in Portugal, especially in the Azores, and in New England before settling in California. There is also a cross section of other ethnic groups in the fishing industry. Sociologically the tuna fishing industry is made up of familial clans who regard fishing as a way of life to be passed on from father to son.[5] Technologically, however, the industry is characterized by modern, sophisticated gear and fishing techniques, as well as by businesslike attitudes. In short it is a big, modern business anchored to "way of life" traditions of earlier fishing patterns.

The U.S. tuna industry has been involved in its own
economic revolution. It modernized itself within a very
short time to become the most profitable fishery of the
United States. With the possible exception of the shrimp
industry, the modernization is unique in U.S. fisheries.
The other U.S. fisheries are small, outdated, inefficient
and unable to compete effectively with foreign fisheries.
To understand these changes one must first understand the
economic patterns previously established in the U.S. tuna
industry.

The tuna industry is composed of three basic components: independent boatowners, fishermen, and canneries.
The tuna fleet is largely privately owned, although some
canneries now have interests in small fleets. Technical-
ly, in the past, the fleet and the canneries were separate
economic entities. However, because of the risky nature
of fishing and the high costs of modernization, the canneries exercised considerable control over the boatowners
either through traditional, paternal relationships or contracted sales. The canneries also have been the source
of financial incentives, and frequently have paved the way
for basic financing.[6] In addition sometimes ethnic bonds
strengthened this relationship.[7] The close relationship
between the boatowners and the canneries benefited both
sides; it provided a market for the fishermen and boatowners and it supplied raw material for the canneries.

The canneries negotiated a contract price for raw
tuna prior to the beginning of a new fishing year. This
price was accepted by both the boatowners and the fishermen's unions. In this sort of bargaining the canneries
generally held the upper hand, controlling both the volume and the prices of the supplies.[8] The fleet owners
tried various tactics to increase their bargaining position. Prior to 1967 the American Tunaboat Association
(ATA), an organization of independent boatowners, had
negotiated the basic contract price on behalf of its members. Because of its growing concern about the seizures
and other political problems, the ATA wished to concentrate on "political" goals rather than economic ones. In
1967, therefore, the American Tuna Sales Association
(ATSA), an association of boatowners and fishermen, was
established to handle the "business" end of the fleet:
pricing the fish, promoting exports, and increasing new
domestic markets.[9]

From 1967 to 1968 the ATSA adopted an "empty boat"
auction for selling catches to the canneries. This means
that the prospective catches are "sold" before the boats

sail so that the individual boatowner does not negotiate singly with the cannery while his boat is idle in port.[10] To get the canneries to accept this system, the boats remained in port 14 weeks in the 1967-68 period. This pattern continues today, with the boatowners and fishermen typically threatening not to sail during December unless the canneries increase their contract price for raw tuna.

Traditionally crew members receive a share of the proceeds of the catch rather than wages or salaries; economically the fishermen are partners in a joint venture rather than employees. Net profits are determined by deducting trip expenses from gross profits. The dividing of the boat's income is under collective bargaining agreement between the boatowner and the union. There is little room for dispute over wages because they are worked out in the traditional formula of "boat shares." Even though the unions participate in the contract bargaining and have some voice in the acceptance of the price, the price of tuna is not really controlled by labor or management.[11] This method of deriving fishermen's wages provides an insight into the economic concern that the fishermen have over boat seizures. All trip expenses--including costs of a seizure--are deducted from the gross profits before dividing the boat's income.

The relations between the canneries and the boatowners have undergone some change in the last few years. In their concern for stable supplies the canneries have become more closely involved with the fleet. They have been buying interests in boats as well as making loans to boatowners for new vessel construction. This means that there has been some reduction in the number of independent boatowners, which has reduced the effectiveness of the auction.

The structure and physical description of the U.S. tuna fleet has changed markedly since the 1950s. The size and capacity of the boats have increased greatly. In addition fishing techniques have changed, requiring extensive investment in new equipment and nets. For example a tuna clipper now may cost a maximum of $3 million, with as much as $90,000 invested in nets.[12]

Fisheries economists point out that the resource is a "common property" that has no single owner with interests to protect, i.e., to prevent overfishing. No one collects an economic rent with which to provide this protection. In fisheries competition the economic rent is divided among all fishermen exploiting the resource. This calls for increasingly heavy capital investment in more sophisticated boats and gear. Not only do costs skyrocket, but excess capacity is created and there is a strong tendency to deplete the resource.[13]

The U.S. tuna industry fits this economic model. The early U.S. bait boats that began fishing off the Galápagos Islands in the 1930s were small and inefficient for long voyages. Their technique was to fish with pole and line after attracting schools of fish with cut bait-fish previously caught close to shore. Now the bait boats have been replaced almost entirely by large, expensive vessels called tuna clippers, which use the purse seine technique of spreading a huge net around a school of fish near the surface. The average vessel now displaces 400 tons and costs some $800,000.[14] It is equipped with sonar and power blocks that lift the nets out of the sea. Some even use spotter planes to locate fish. The success of the U.S. tuna fishing techniques has persuaded some of the world's major maritime nations, such as Japan, Canada, and the Soviet Union, to consider adoption of purse seining for tuna.

Species

There are several varieties of tuna, differing in terms of lightness, desirability, and price. Albacore, the prime white-meat fish, is caught by small coastal boats along the California and Mexican coast, or is imported from Japan. Approximately 15 percent of U.S. tuna landings are albacore. The next species is the yellowfin tuna found in the South Pacific and Central Pacific. It is the lightest of three varieties of tuna found in the same waters; this means that it is the highest priced. The next lightest is the bluefin tuna. Finally there is the skipjack tuna, darker and smaller than the other species, but more abundant. The ratio of these species in the 1967 Pacific Coast landings was albacore, 15.4 percent; yellowfin, 45 percent; skipjack, 35.2 percent; and bluefin, 4.4 percent.[15]

In 1966 the Inter-American Tropical Tuna Commission (I-ATTC) began establishing a quota on the amount of yellowfin tuna taken from the Eastern Pacific. This organization was begun in 1949 by the United States and Costa Rica to gather scientific information on conservation of tuna and its bait-fish. Other nations that currently participate in the commission are Canada, Mexico, Panama, Japan, and Colombia. None of the CEP nations are members, although Ecuador joined for a brief period.

The I-ATTC functions as an international conservation agreement that sets species quotas rather than national catch quotas.[16] Since 1966 the open season for yellowfin tuna in the Eastern Pacific, established by the agreement, has been starting on January 1 and continuing until the quota is filled with the combined catches of all nations fishing in the zone. This means that fishermen participate in an international race to catch yellowfin before the end of the season. The duration of the season has been getting progressively shorter; in 1966 it ended in September, but in 1972 it ended in March. Once the yellowfin season ends, the tuna fleet turns to fishing for skipjack. The race for yellowfin indicates why seizures seem to occur either early or late in the year. If the fish are running off Ecuador and Peru during the season, the boats will be there. At the end of the year the boat-owners may decide to make one more trip into the disputed waters before returning to their home port to prepare for the next yellowfin season.[17] The 1972 quota was established at 120,000 tons with an additional 20,000 tons for incidental catches. The U.S. fleet catches about 90 percent of the total quota, which means that U.S. fishermen feel that the conservation restrictions apply primarily to them. They frequently charge that the fishermen of other nations, whether or not they are members of the I-ATTC, disregard the quota system.[18] It has also been pointed out, however, that sometimes the total yellowfin catch, including the incidental allowance, is as much as 8 percent higher than the maximum sustainable catch recommended scientifically.[19]

Skipjack is a smaller, more abundant species. Fishing for skipjack is easier and does not require the high degree of skill necessary for successful yellowfin fishing; and since the mercury scare of 1970 fishermen have regarded catching skipjack somewhat more favorably. Despite skipjack's lower price, its smaller size makes it less likely to be contaminated with a high mercury content. The fleet's efforts to catch skipjack are quite wide-ranging. Many vessels are currently fishing in the Central Pacific where they are able to offload their catches at the two U.S. canneries in Samoa. There are also some vessels, about 32 currently, which have turned to fishing off the African coast in the South Atlantic. These vessels obviously find it more convenient to offload in Puerto Rico.

Fishing Techniques

There are three ways of catching tuna: bait boat fishing, which characterized the U.S. tuna industry before 1958; purse seining, which is the technique currently used by the U.S. tuna fleet; and longline fishing. Longline fishing involves miles of line with thousands of hoods attached; this type of gear is favored by the Japanese fleet. Contrary to the bait boat and the purse seine, the long-line catches those tuna swimming beneath the surface. The most efficient of the three techniques is the purse seine. After the introduction of nylon nets in the late 1950s, with the use of a power block for net retrieval, this technique provided the ability to catch many more fish per set. The seiners are also relieved of the necessity of catching live bait. The efficiency of the new technique was so apparent that within three years, between 1958 and 1961, the U.S. tuna fleet transformed itself from a bait boat fleet to a purse seine fleet.[20] Seining increased a vessel's productivity and its earnings potential, and reduced the length of a typical voyage as well.[21] In addition the increased efficiency meant that the U.S. fishermen could compete with foreign imports.[22]

Profits

The economic problem of the boatowners is not return on investment. A study prepared for the Department of Commerce gathered figures on the financial performance of the average 400-ton, $800,000 seiner at 1969 prices. These show that a boat can gross $516,865 per year by making five or six successful fishing trips. The average annual expenses for such a vessel were figured at $387,946, including the crew's compensation. Each of the 11 to 13 crew members on this vessel would earn between $15,000 and $20,000 annually, with additional bonuses for the captain, engineer, mastman, and deck boss. The boatowner would net $128,929 before depreciation and taxes, or a rate of return on investment of 16.1 percent.[23] This financial performance is adequately rewarding, so that, given the nature of competitive fishing, costs will continue to rise and profits will continue to fall as new entrants are attracted to the fishery.

Since these economic consultants believe that the basic problem of the boatowners and fishermen is lack of control over marketing of their product, the report suggests that the boatowners abandon the auction system, pool their catches, process them in a cooperative transshipment and storage plant, and then market them to all potential buyers including canneries outside Southern California. The report concludes that unless they do this, they will never have adequate control over the price and volume of their products. There are several obstacles to acceptance of these suggestions. The canneries naturally oppose them. In addition the suggestions require that the boatowner give up his vaunted "independence" in selling his catch by promising to sell to the marketing organization.[24]

Cannery Location

Until quite recently California canneries dominated the U.S. production of canned tuna, especially those located in San Pedro and San Diego. As recently as the late 1950s, California had over 20 tuna canneries, which canned most of the U.S. production--three of them accounted for about two-thirds of the total pack.[25] This pattern has changed considerably since then. Currently five major canneries have opened new facilities in Puerto Rico and construction of another is under consideration. These canneries have several advantages: they can distribute their pack to the eastern United States more cheaply; they can export canned tuna to the growing European market more cheaply; and they are closer to the sources of supply of raw tuna, both the new fishing grounds off Africa and the Ecuadorian and Peruvian exports of frozen tuna. In addition a major lure in the relocation of cannery facilities is the availability of a cheaper supply of labor. This means that the fishermen and boatowners are less concerned about the relocation than are the unionized cannery workers. There are also two new fish canneries in Samoa. The combined output of the U.S. canneries outside California accounted for about 56 percent of the total tuna pack in 1971, with the California output at 44 percent.[26]

The impact of the cannery relocation is multiple. Thirty-nine of the newer, most modern seiners have followed the canneries to Puerto Rico and are based there permanently. This pattern affects the jobs of California fishermen as well as those of cannery workers. Some have been concerned that this pattern may accelerate, or even that the boatowners will base and staff their vessels in

Latin America in order to avoid the problems of seizures and other harassment. The relocations have had different impacts on San Diego and San Pedro. Currently San Pedro has three canneries, but only 13 tuna boats are based there, while San Diego has only one cannery with approximately 71 tuna boats based there. San Diego is trying to encourage the establishment of another major cannery in its area. Because of the new fishing grounds discovered in the Central Pacific,[27] San Diego officials rationalize that there is a valid reason for the continuation of San Diego as an important center of the U.S. tuna industry. Another impact of the cannery transfers is the increased flexibility to boats in terms of offloading. A vessel can fish the Eastern Pacific during the yellowfin season and offload either in Puerto Rico or Southern California. Then it can either fish in the Central Pacific and possibly offload in Samoa, or go to the Atlantic where it can offload in Puerto Rico.[28]

International Demand

There is growing international demand for tuna, which maintains high prices and stimulates boat construction. The ATA is very concerned about the subsidies used by other nations to promote their tuna fleets. During the American occupation of Japan the fishing industry was promoted as official policy. Since that time the Japanese government has promoted its fishing industry, primarily by insured, low-interest loans, in order to increase food supplies and to build foreign exchange. For example the General Fishing Agency of Japan authorized the construction of 563 steel ships with a total of 107,242 gross tons and 212 wooden ships with a total of 7,077 gross tons in 1969 alone--all built for the tuna fishery. By 1972 Japan had some 3,000 registered tuna vessels.[29] They are obviously small boats using the longline fishing technique. Several other nations, including Korea and Taiwan, also are subsidizing vessel construction to expand their own tuna fleets.

Licenses

License costs to fish the waters claimed by Ecuador and Peru are based on vessel size. For example a 50-day Ecuadorian license costs $20 per ton, or about $8,000 for an average-sized fishing boat. The rate of fines is set

at a maximum of five times the cost of the license. New
fishing regulations in Peru stipulate that foreign vessels
must pay $20 per ton on their catches plus a $500 fee for
fishing permits.[30] Peruvian fines have generally been
modest compared to Ecuadorian fines. Ecuador fined the
largest seiner, the _Apollo_, twice in 1971. On her maiden
voyage the 1,800 ton, $3 million vessel was seized and
fined $86,650, but was released with her $700,000 catch
and allowed to return to her home port in Puerto Rico. A
few weeks later the _Apollo_ was seized again and fined
$157,740. The ATA believes that the second seizure oc-
curred because the captain had testified about the first
seizure before a hearing of the House Committee on Merchant Marine and Fisheries.[31] On the occasion of the latter seizure the captain was warned that if the vessel were
caught again, it might be confiscated outright and turned
over to Ecuador's own tuna fleet. Its license cost at the
$20 per ton rate would be $36,000. But under normal fishing conditions a 50-day license would not be long enough
for such a large vessel to fill its capacity. Some boatowners have indicated that they would not mind paying a
"reasonable" license fee if the time period were long
enough to insure a full load on one license.[32]

It should be pointed out that there have always been
a few U.S. tuna vessels that have bought licenses. In the
first place the remaining bait boats continue to buy licenses as they have always done because catching bait fish
requires them to operate within three miles of the coast.
There are also a few boatowners who buy licenses for economic reasons--they could not afford the short-run financial costs of the fines in terms of burdensome high-
interest loans. In addition there were two vessels that
bought 1972 licenses on the advice of the ATA; they had
been singled out because of past seizures or because of
their captain's public statements. In this case the reasons for buying licenses involved a desire to avoid financially punitive fines as well as to insure the safety of
the crew. The ATA does not believe that the voluntary
purchase of licenses is increasing. A few boats have
bought, and probably will continue to buy, licenses for
specific reasons. The boatowners remain convinced for the
time being that, apart from these exceptional cases, voluntary purchase would set a precedent that all the nations
up and down the Eastern Pacific coast might insist upon.[33]

Imports and Tariffs

The California canneries began importing frozen albacore from Japan in the late 1920s. Since World War II,
however, the imports have included significant amounts of
tuna as well. In its efforts to rebuild the Japanese
economy after the war the U.S. government encouraged the
rebuilding of the Japanese fishing industry. The rapidly
rising U.S. demand for tuna caused the rapid increase of
tuna imports. For example 7.5 percent of U.S. tuna consumption was imported in 1947; in ten years this figure
had grown to 46 percent.[34] Initially the canners regarded
these imports as supplementary supplies. After a record
catch in 1950 depressed prices, however, the canners began
to regulate their purchase of domestic catches rather than
imports, in an effort to control production volume.[35] The
canners benefited from the imports in that they provided
price competition for raw tuna and an alternative source
of supply.

U.S. tuna boats freeze their catches without processing them in any way. This means that they are not brought
to the canneries at maximum value. The imported tuna is
cleaned, gutted, and frequently precooked in can-shaped
discs. This means that it can demand a higher price--
possibly 40 percent higher--than the domestic catch.[36]
Presumably the higher costs are offset by savings in processing costs.

In the early 1950s there were two primary sources for
the tuna imports--Japan and Peru. Japan's reentry into
the world tuna fishery was an integral part of rebuilding
a viable economy, and as such had the support of the State
Department. Peru had expanded its tuna fishing during
World War II in order to meet the U.S. demand. The United
States began importing frozen Peruvian tuna in 1948 and by
1951 the value of such imports was more than $800,000.[37]

The vast increase of imports stimulated demands by
the U.S. boatowners and fishermen in the early 1950s that
tariffs or quotas be imposed on imports. In 1952 these
demands persuaded the House of Representatives to pass
a three cent per pound tariff on imported raw tuna. There
was strong opposition to the tariff from the canneries,
the proponents of free trade, and the State Department.
The proposal failed to pass the Senate. Since that time
other proposals to reduce tuna imports have been ignored.
Now of course the modern U.S. purse seiners are more able
to compete with imports than the bait boats were.

Although there is no tariff on raw tuna, there are tariffs on other forms of tuna. Frozen raw tuna is duty free and always has been. Frozen cooked tuna in can-shaped discs became important imports after 1952. The rate of duty on them is 1¢ per pound. Since they have an average foreign value of 24¢ to 40¢ per pound, the duty is equivalent to 2.25-4 percent ad valorem. Tuna canned in oil had a duty of 30 percent ad valorem under the 1930 Tariff Act. This rate increased to 45 percent ad valorem in 1934. It was reduced to 22.5 percent in a 1943 trade agreement with Mexico; when that agreement terminated in 1951, the rate reverted to the 45 percent rate. Then in 1955, in a concession originally negotiated with Japan, the rate on tuna canned in oil was reduced to 35 percent ad valorem, which continues to be the current rate.

The United States also imports tuna canned in brine. This product became an important import in 1951 when the rate on tuna canned in oil increased. In fact this product now comprises almost all the canned tuna imported into the United States. The rate on tuna canned in brine, as es-tablished in the General Agreement on Tariffs and Trade (GATT) after negotiations with Japan, is a maximum of 12.5 percent ad valorem on all imports under 20 percent of U.S. production of canned tuna during the preceding calendar year. The excess of the quota is dutiable, by presiden-tial decree, at 25 percent ad valorem.[38] Under the Kennedy Round of negotiations, the tariff rates on tuna canned in brine have decreased from the 12.5 percent in effect before 1968 to 6 percent in 1972. The 1972 quota allows 78,531,760 pounds of tuna canned in brine to be im-ported at the 6 percent ad valorem rate. Amounts in ex-cess of the quota have a duty of 12.5 percent ad valorem.[39]

THE U.S. TUNA INDUSTRY AS A PRESSURE GROUP

Despite the fragmented economic sectors within the tuna industry, politically the industry's primary spokes-man is the ATA. Clearly the ATA fits Gabriel Almond's definition of an associational interest group--it formu-lates interests and demands and transmits these demands to other political structures, such as parties, legisla-tures, and bureaucracies.[40] However, the organization maintains no lobbyists in Washington, has no public rela-tions operation, and maintains a rather modest budget said to be less than $150,000 per year.[41] Such departures from our traditional expectations about important interest groups have not reduced the ATA's effectiveness. The ATA has effective access to sympathetic congressmen—this serves in lieu of other more apparent lobbying operations.

The ATA's activities have been designed both to promote the tuna industry and to get action in solving the problem of seizures. In the past the ATA has been extremely effective in the use of the mass media to influence wide public support for the boatowners and fishermen in the dispute over territorial waters. A major effort of the ATA has been directed at political-legislative goals. Its spokesmen have testified repeatedly at public hearings. They have been in close contact with legislators, especially the senators and representatives from California and those members of the congressional committees that deal with fisheries. During times of special crisis over the seizures ATA officers and members have maintained daily contact with congressional supporters, as well as with the fisheries experts in the Departments of State and Commerce. For example, in a memorandum of February 16, 1969, the ATA's general manager detailed his activities at the time of the San Juan shooting incident. After receiving word that the vessel was being pursued and fired upon, he first contacted the State Department's fisheries expert. Then he contacted the offices of San Diego Congressman Bob Wilson and Senators George Murphy and Alan Cranston, both of California. He also received numerous calls from the mass media about the episode.[42]

The ATA also has collected and disseminated a variety of factual information about the tuna industry, the nature of tuna, and, most especially, the seizures. Since 1961, when it became apparent that the seizures were not merely a temporary aberration, the ATA has maintained detailed records of the seizures: names and locations of the vessels that have been seized, dates they were held, and the amounts paid in fees and fines. Another activity of the ATA has been its participation in a variety of official and unofficial diplomatic efforts to solve the issues of conservation, seizure, licenses, and territorial limits.

The activities of the ATA have had several specific goals. Recently they have been trying to make clear that what the press refers to as the "tuna war" is not a struggle between the tuna industry and Ecuador, but is really a boundary dispute between the United States and the 200-mile claimants. They also emphasize the migratory nature of tuna in an international fishery, publicizing the fact that a claim to national ownership of any of the species in a particular zone is unrealistic biologically as well as legally. Another point which the ATA has stressed is that the scarcest species, the yellowfin, is protected under an international conservation agreement, the I-ATTC, to which the United States and its fishermen adhere, but which the claiming nations ignore.[43] In legislative terms the ATA has been steady in its demands for retaliatory legislation to punish the nations that seize U.S. fishing boats. This is true even though the exercise of the sanctions has escalated the seizures. The specific nature of these retaliatory laws and proposals is discussed later in this chapter.

The ATA has aimed its activities at elite opinion (legislators and the administration) and at mass public opinion. Until quite recently there was extensive press coverage of the seizure incidents, particularly in Southern California. In 1972 and 1973 there was less coverage. This reduced attention to the increased seizures may be an example of Bernard Cohen's theories of mass media and foreign policy. Cohen discovered that the mass media cover only one "big story" at a time, with "lesser" stories treated in a subordinate manner. If the conception of the big story changes, continued episodes in its development may not be covered even though they appear to be of the same weight and a continuation of those that were previously covered. Cohen believes that newsworthiness is determined by such criteria as "drama" and ideas about what interests the public. This process becomes a self-fulfilling prophecy; if a subject is not covered, the public will not be interested.[44] Thus it may be that the very repetition, and even the escalation, of the seizures, has caused the media to perceive them as routine occurrences, and therefore not newsworthy. The ATA maintains that its activities and policies about publicizing the seizures have not changed. Its press releases apparently are ignored, however, and it is not contacted by the media about the most recent seizures.

Legislator Response

A small number of elected politicians, especially those from California and those who are members of congressional fisheries committees, have been very responsive to the pressures of the tuna industry. In fact some have welcomed the issue of seizures, for several reasons. Obviously the politicians and the general public alike are frustrated with foreign policy problems and desire simple answers and conclusive solutions for them. The seizures have allowed them to vent some of this frustration in a manner that they have perceived to be acceptable and un-embarrassing to the general goals of U.S. foreign policy. Clearly, however, this has been a false perception.

Second, the seizures have permitted the legislators and the interest group to berate the State Department for its alleged "softness" in protecting the interests of the fishermen, which they believe to be the same as the inter-ests of the United States. Several congressmen have been bitter because the State Department sometimes has avoided application of the retaliatory legislation. The attitude has been that the State Department has the tuna industry in the grips of a "Catch 22" rule. The State Department advises the fishermen not to purchase licenses to avoid tantamount recognition of the 200-mile claim--advice with which the tuna industry agrees--but at the same time has been unable to prevent the seizures. These two "failures" of the State Department--the failure to apply the retalia-tory legislation and the failure to solve the dispute or prevent seizures--have caused some legislators to attack the department as "inactive."[45]

Finally the issue of seizures has allowed the legis-lators to be responsive to the parochial economic inter-ests of their state or district. In fact for some legis-lators the issue of seizures is superior to most parochial economic issues because of its "patriotic" appearance. It allows the legislator to drape himself in the flag, de-nouncing the loss of the worthy traditions of "interna-tional law" and "freedom of the seas," while pressing for the actions demanded by the tuna industry. For example one congressman said that although "Chicken of the Sea" was a respected name in the tuna industry, it should not characterize American "protection" of its tuna fleet.[46] In other words the issue of seizures has allowed the sym-pathetic legislators to curry favor with the tuna industry by acting as foreign policy "hard-liners."

The congressmen who represent San Diego and San Pedro naturally have been major spokesmen for the tuna industry. Since they are long-time legislators, the relationship be-tween them and the tuna industry is well established. They are Representatives Wilson and Lionel Van Deerlin, both of San Diego, and Representative Glenn M. Anderson of San Pedro. California senators also have sponsored legislative proposals favored by the tuna interests. Perhaps the fore-most legislative spokesman for the industry has been Repre-sentative Thomas Pelly, who represents a Washington district

in which fishing--though not tuna fishing--is important.
Pelly is the ranking Republican member of the House Committee on Merchant Marine and Fisheries. He has been very
active in introducing a wide variety of retaliatory legislative proposals favored by the tuna industry. Even
though the Pelly amendments are widely condemned in Latin
America, Pelly himself is proud to take credit for most of
the sanctions on the statute books that deal with seizures.[47]

Legislation

In 1954 the Fishermen's Protective Act was passed.
Introduced by Representative Wilson, the act provided
that the fines would be reimbursed to the boatowners by
the federal government. The act directed the secretary
of state to attend to the welfare of any U.S.-flag vessel
and crew seized by a foreign country in international
waters. If a license fee or fine was imposed, the act
directed the secretary of the treasury to reimburse the
owners in the amount certified by the secretary of state
as being the amount actually paid, provided there was no
dispute on material facts relating to the vessel's loca-
tion or activities at the time of seizure.[48] The reaction of the claimant nations to this legislation was that
it encouraged the fishermen to violate their national
laws.

As the seizures began to increase, the boatowners
began accruing losses beyond those of fees or fines, including confiscated or spoiled catches and valuable lost
fishing time. Therefore the Fishermen's Protective Act
of 1967, passed August 12, 1968, provided government sub-
sidy for these losses through a financial assistance program.[49] This program was administered by the Bureau of
Commercial Fisheries of the Interior Department until
1970, when the bureau was transferred to the Department
of Commerce. Because of this transfer the 1967 act authorizes the secretary of commerce to make a guarantee
agreement with the owners of U.S.-flag vessels, guaranteeing to reimburse them for all actual costs incurred
during seizure and detention. These losses include damage to the vessel or its gear, confiscation of the vessel, gear, or equipment, and dockage fees. It also guarantees reimbursement of the market value of the fish
losses as a result of confiscation or spoilage. It further provides for reimbursement to the owner and crew of

up to 50 percent of the gross income lost as a direct result of the seizure or detention. The full amount of the
loss was not covered because it was felt that the fishermen might deliberately provoke seizure otherwise. In order for a boatowner to enter into a guarantee agreement,
a fee is charged based on anticipated losses, administrative costs, and one-third of the estimated claims. The
remaining two-thirds is provided by the U.S. Treasury.
Originally the reimbursement feature of the act was a four-
year program, ending in February 1973. In a 1972 amendment, however, these provisions were extended until July 1,
1977.[50] The guarantee agreement program was promoted by
the tuna industry and has been enthusiastically supported
by it. Recently, however, in view of the potential seizures of U.S.-owned, distant-water shrimp boats in the
Caribbean and the Gulf of Mexico, as well as in the new
Brazilian claim area, significant numbers of shrimp vessel
operators also participate.[51]

Another provision of the law, a Pelly amendment,
directs the secretary of state to try to collect the
amounts fined through claims against the nation that
seized the vessel; the secretary of state "shall take
such action as he may deem appropriate to make and collect
claims against a foreign country" for the amounts reimbursed to the fishermen. If the claims are not paid within 120 days, a like amount shall be withheld from the current foreign aid programmed for that nation. Because the
State Department has not "deemed it appropriate," it has
never filed such a claim with a nation that has seized
U.S. fishing boats. This means of course that it has
never deducted the amount of the fines from foreign aid
programmed for a country. The position of the State Department is that the imposition of this sanction would
not further the chances of negotiating a solution to the
dispute. Representative Pelly and others who favor exercising sanctions are exasperated by the State Department's
"inactivity."[52]

In addition to the Fishermen's Protective Acts the
tuna interests have also promoted several laws that punish
the nations responsible for the seizures. These include
the following:

1. Foreign Assistance Act of 1956 as amended by the
"Kuchel Amendment" in 1965.[53] This amendment provides
that seizures will be taken into account in determining
whether a nation will receive foreign aid. Since the
amendment leaves this determination to the discretion of
the Secretary of State, its provisions have never been

applied. For a brief period in 1969, however, the State Department did warn Ecuador and Peru that it could be applied. When those nations countered by threatening to boycott inter-American meetings and fishery negotiations, the threat was dropped.

2. Naval Vessels Loan Extension Act of 1967.[54] This act provided that any vessels provided in a government-to-government loan must be recalled if the borrowing nation is responsible for "illegal" seizures. This measure also provides for executive discretion. The irony of this measure is that none of the vessels in the Ecuadorian navy were covered by this law. Ecuador has two vessels that were originally part of a government-to-government loan, but that loan expired in 1965, and Ecuador, like the other "borrowers" have done, merely kept the vessels without a new loan agreement.

3. Foreign Military Sales Act of 1968 as amended by a Pelly amendment.[55] This amendment provided that no military weapons or goods may be sold to any nation responsible for seizures, although it too provides for presidential waiver. This provision was applied to Ecuador after several seizures had occurred in 1971, and Ecuador countered by bringing charges of "economic coercion" against the United States in the OAS and evicting the U.S. military missions in Ecuador. Ecuador insists that she will not reenter fisheries negotiations until this sanction is lifted. In an interesting footnote to the application of this sanction Representative Pelly himself asked President Nixon to waive its application after relations between Ecuador and the United States became so strained.[56]

4. Foreign Assistance Appropriations Act of 1972 as amended by the Van Deerlin amendment.[57] This amendment prohibited any appropriations contained in the act from being granted to Ecuador, although it also provided for presidential waiver if the president "determines that such assistance is important to the national interest of the United States." Ecuador's delegate to the U.N. Committee on Peaceful Uses of the Seabed denounced the legislation as "shameful and discriminatory" and the "purest form of imperialism." This protest was supported by the delegates from Chile, Peru, Brazil, and China.[58]

There have been a variety of other retaliatory proposals that failed to pass. Generally they have involved either proposed embargoes on the seizing nations or cancellations of some form of U.S. aid to the seizing nations. For example in 1969 Congressman Pelly introduced H.R. 10607, which would have prohibited the importation of fish products from a nation that illegally seizes U.S. fishing vessels.[59] The ATA believes that the threat implicit in this proposal was an important stimulus in getting the quadripartite fisheries negotiations started. Another example was an amendment to S. 748, the Inter-American Development Bank (I-ADB) Act, introduced by Representative Glenn Anderson, which provided that the United States vote against the extension of any I-ADB loans to a nation that had seized U.S. vessels. Although this amendment passed in the House of Representatives, it was ultimately deleted from the I-ADB Act.[60]

There have been a number of other possible retaliations mentioned in floor speeches or congressional resolutions. Periodically reduction of the sugar quota has been mentioned as a potential retaliation. There have been repeated demands, sometimes in legislative proposals, that coast guard escorts be provided for the tuna fleet. Another example was the 1969 resolution introduced by the chairman of the House Committee on Merchant Marine and Fisheries, Edward Garmatz, and others asking the president not to lend Peru a destroyer that had been authorized in P.L. 90-224, and to request the return of a vessel whose loan had expired.

It should be made clear that although the ATA is the major lobby for the tuna industry, it is by no means the only one. The fishermen's unions--the Seafarer's International Union (AFL-CIO) and the Fishermen and Allied Workers' Union, Local 33 (ILWU)--as well as the cannery workers' union, United Cannery and Industrial Workers of the Pacific (SIU, AFL-CIO), have been very outspoken in demanding protection for the fishing boats and retaliation for the seizures. In fact these unions cooperated in 1971 in staging a brief boycott against the unloading of an Ecuadorian banana boat. Other organizations include the ATSA, the Tuna Research Foundation, the Western Fishboats Association, and the Women's League for Fishermen's Rights. The latter organization, composed of the wives and daughters of fishermen, picketed and demonstrated at the office of the Ecuadorian consul in Los Angeles in January 1971.

A major concern of the ATA recently has been to speed the reimbursement of the fines and seizure costs to the boatowners. In 1972 Congressman Pelly introduced a measure, H.R. 7117, to expedite the reimbursement procedures.[61] The average waiting period from the time of seizure to reimbursement was 430 days, during which time the owner's capital was depleted and he was paying a high rate of interest on the money borrowed to secure the release of his vessel.

The reimbursement process was lengthy for several reasons. In the first place the Fishermen's Protective Act of 1967 requires the secretary of state to have complete data about the vessel, the seizure, and the catch, among other data, before it certifies the claim to the secretary of the treasury. After this certification the funds for the purpose of reimbursement must be allocated in a supplemental appropriation measure passed by Congress. In order to speed this process H.R. 7117 proposed the establishment of a $3 million Fishermen's Protective Fund. The secretary of state is required to ascertain immediately the amount paid by the owner for release of his vessel, for immediate rèimbursement by the secretary of the treasury.

Besides speeding the reimbursement procedure, H.R. 7117 was frankly designed to compel the State Department to cancel foreign aid to the seizing nations in an amount equal to the reimbursements. The operative language was to require the secretary of state to notify the seizing country immediately of a reimbursement claim and to take appropriate action to collect the amount of the claim from the offending country. The reduction of foreign aid must go into effect 120 days after notification rather than after the filing of a claim. The State Department opposed these features of the bill as abrasive and potentially escalatory. Nonetheless the measure was finally adopted in October 1972.[62]

California's Senators Tunney and Cranston introduced a proposal, S. 1242, in 1971 to amend the Fishermen's Protective Act of 1967 to cover the costs involved in attempted as well as actual seizures. Because of the difficulties in defining an "attempted seizure" and in verifying it, this measure failed to receive any serious consideration.[63]

The tuna industry also lobbied vigorously on the Marine Mammal Protection Act of 1972. Because tuna travel in close association with porpoises, many thousands of porpoises drown in the nets of the purse seiners. In fact federal officials estimate that 315,000 porpoises died in tuna seines in 1970 and 205,000 died in 1971.[64] Tuna fishermen locate the tuna schools by first locating the porpoises on the surface. When the seines are drawn in, the porpoises frequently panic, entangle themselves in the four-inch net, and drown. This happens even though the boats employ a technique called "backing down," which allows the mammals to escape. Sometimes fishermen even jump into the nets to release them. In 1971 Harold Medina, captain of the Kerri M, tried a new, smaller mesh panel in the seine and determined that this modification made it more

difficult for the porpoises to become entangled. The tuna
fishermen maintain that the Medina panels will help reduce
porpoise deaths to minimal numbers. They also believe
that the use of the panels will reduce the time needed for
sets, thus increasing efficiency.[65]

The tuna industry vigorously opposed a moratorium on
porpoise deaths "incidental" to tuna seining, maintaining
that porpoises are essential for successful purse seining,
and that therefore they will go to great lengths to avoid
porpoise deaths. The ATA retained a marine science consult-
ing company, Living Marine Resources, Inc. to study the
porpoise deaths and the effectiveness of the Medina panels
in conserving porpoise stocks.[66] These efforts were successful in avoiding the most sweeping prohibitions of the
Marine Mammal Act. The commercial fishing ventures were
given a two-year exemption, with possible extensions, from
the moratorium on the "taking of marine mammals." Furthermore the administration of porpoise conservation was given
to the Department of Commerce rather than the Department of
the Interior.[67] An editorial in the New York _Times_ charged
that this was because the Department of Commerce was pro-
industry in its attitude while the Department of the Interior had a strong conservationist tradition.[68] The Commerce Department's National Oceanic and Atmospheric Administration is encouraging the fishermen to adopt the Medina
panels. It is also conducting further studies of the porpoise population, the number of "incidental" porpoise
deaths, and new fishing gear or techniques that might contribute to saving porpoises.

This catalogue of demanded and enacted legislation
illustrates that the tuna industry has been effective in
Washington considering its relative size and budget. However, certain other things are apparent as well. Some
legislators seem determined to enhance their own careers
by sponsoring legislation, because it is equally clear
that much of the legislation has done nothing to promote
solution to the dispute. In fact the retaliatory legislation, though designed to salve the resentments of the tuna
industry, merely served to inflame and aggravate the entire question for the Latin American nations, without
pacifying the tuna industry.

Charles Goodsell uses the 1969 Peruvian fisheries
crisis to show that what he calls the "forceful interposition type of diplomatic protection" was counterproductive.[69] During the heightened diplomatic tensions over
the International Petroleum Corporation dispute, renewed
fishing boat seizures outraged the U.S. tuna industry,

provoking demands for forceful government action. Representative Pelly arranged for the industry leaders to meet with the undersecretary of state for Latin America and other officials of the State Department. On the heels of this meeting the United States lodged formal protests with the Peruvian government and warned that a destroyer on loan might be recalled if the $50,000 damage to the San Juan were not repaid by the Peruvians. The United States also secretly suspended military sales to Peru as provided by the Pelly amendment to the Foreign Military Sales Act. Additional seizures prompted disgruntled congressmen to reveal the secret ban on military sales. At that point, according to Goodsell's analysis, the junta had no alternative but to react harshly. It pleaded ignorance of the sanction, evicted the U.S. military missions, and canceled Governor Rockefeller's visit as "inopportune." A month later the United States agreed to lift the ban on military sales in return for Peruvian attendance at the quadripartite fisheries negotiations in Buenos Aires. Those negotiations, however, produced no change in the 200-mile claims.

Paradoxically the counterproductivity of the "forceful interposition" type of diplomacy is not apparent to the tuna interests. They interpret the failure as one caused by the State Department's inaction, foot-dragging, and unwillingness to protect the interests of the fishing industry. Their problem involved an unwillingness to recognize that the locus of decision-making is not in the domestic scene, where they have considerable power, but in the domestic and international politics of foreign nations, where their power is limited. In fact it is true that the power of the tuna industry in the domestic scene contributes to its problems. The Peruvian and Ecuadorian governments are not inclined to halt the seizures or reduce the claim if they believe that U.S. foreign policy is a tool of special interests. The domestic power of the tuna interests reinforces that perception. Moreover in this case the special interest manipulating U.S. foreign policy is not one that brings any benefits to Ecuador or Peru. The same cannot be said for some other special U.S. interests, such as oil or fishmeal, in Ecuador and Peru.

MULTIPLE INTERESTS AND U.S. FOREIGN POLICY

It has slowly dawned on the California-based tuna industry that the United States has multiple and conflicting interests involved in the complex questions of international law of the sea, territorial waters, fishery conservation, and hemispheric goodwill. It has already been explained that within the tuna industry itself there are fragmented economic sectors--boatowners, canneries, and fishermen; canneries located in Southern California, Puerto Rico, and Samoa; and U.S. firms with interests in the Ecuadorian and Peruvian tuna industries. Fishing corporations with multinational interests--Van Camp, Del Monte, and Star-Kist--found themselves advising both the U.S. and the Ecuadorian delegations at the 1969 Quadripartite Fisheries Conference in Buenos Aires.

Currently a much more serious fragmentation is that dividing the general U.S. fishing industry on the question of exclusive fishing zones for the United States. The industry is divided according to what species of fish are caught at what distances offshore.

The U.S. fishing industry's two distant-water fisheries--shrimp and tuna--both fish off Latin American coasts. Both are also high investment, high return fisheries. On the other hand, the U.S. coastal fishermen generally are traditional craftsmen using dated, inefficient boats and equipment; they are unable to compete efficiently against the sophisticated fishing industries of other maritime nations. In 1966 the coastal fishing industries were instrumental in pressuring the United States to extend its exclusive fishing zone from three to twelve miles. The distant-water tuna and shrimp industries both opposed this extension because they feared that other nations would follow suit.[70]

The differences within the fishing industry have grown considerably since that time, largely because foreign fishing off U.S. coasts has grown enormously. Japanese and Russian fishing fleets have been active along the Pacific coasts and are blamed for the depleting stocks of several species there. Agitation is much more heated along the Atlantic, where fishing fleets from many other nations fish--the Soviet Union, Poland, East and West Germany, Bulgaria, Spain, Japan, Italy, Norway, Canada, Rumania, and Cuba.[71] Typically these fleets patrol the rich fishing waters above the continental shelf in competition with the coastal U.S. boats. One of the conflicts has been likened to that between the farmers and cattlemen of the Old West. U.S. lobstermen set out lengthy strings of lobster pots and traps that are connected to each other and to surface buoys. The foreign trawlers, however, pursue fish, frequently any and all species, with bottom nets. This means that they frequently have pulled up and destroyed

lobster traps and gear.[72] This is not the only problem, by
any means. Many species caught traditionally by U.S. fishermen are declining rapidly; the number of fishermen able
to support themselves is declining rapidly also. Ironically a number of the fish packing plants are able to survive
only because they buy raw fish from the foreign vessels.

In the past two or three years the coastal fishermen
have reacted to these threats by lobbying for legislative
protection and public support for their plight. Organizations have been formed, including the Emergency Committee
to Save America's Marine Resources and the New England
Fisheries Steering Committee. In February 1972 the Atlantic Offshore Fishermen's Association was formed in order
to unify the efforts of a variety of other groups and fishermen of different species. It employs professional lobbyists in Washington to present claims for damages against
foreign fishermen and to represent the coastal fishermen
to U.S. bureaucracies, the Congress, and foreign governments.[73]

A fishery's position on U.S. fishing policy is determined by species. Generally the ground fishermen support
an extension of the exclusive U.S. fishing zone. One exception is the menhaden industry because this species is
caught quite close to shore. U.S. shrimp fishermen are
divided; some catch local or coastal shrimp and they want
greater protection for "their" coastal shrimp. The
distant-water shrimpers fish near the coasts of a number
of other nations, including Mexico, Guiana, Brazil, and
the Caribbean nations. Some of these shrimp, especially
those off the Brazilian coast, are somewhat more migratory
and deeper-water species than the coastal varieties. The
distant-water shrimping industry therefore opposes a U.S.
extension of its fishing zone for fear it will provoke retaliations in areas where it fishes.

On the Pacific coast the coastal fishermen have ex-
perienced the results of either their own overfishing or
that of the Soviet or Japanese boats. Several species
have virtually disappeared: sardines, Pacific mackerel,
and Pacific Ocean perch. These fishermen support an extension of the exclusive fishing zone. The position of
the Alaskan salmon industry is complicated by the salmon
life cycle. Since salmon are an anadromous species that
return to their spawning grounds, if they were harvested
in order to promote conservation, fishing would be allowed
only near the mouths of the rivers. In that way a controlled number would be certain to reach the spawning
grounds. However, the salmon spend most of their life

cycle well beyond a 200-mile limit, and in fact about 70 percent of the world salmon catch is caught beyond this distance.[74] The salmon industry worries that if the open seas salmon catch continues, there is no means of guaranteeing salmon conservation. For these reasons the salmon industry wants to have complete national control of the salmon harvest.

Clearly the tuna industry faces serious challenges over the direction of U.S. fisheries policies. The segments of the fishing industry may be on a collision course: some fishermen are zealous in demanding an extension up to 200 miles; others want national control over one species for further than 200 miles; and the distant-water fishermen oppose oceanic nationalism and extension of the fishery zone. The California tuna industry has enjoyed considerable political clout in Washington both because of the state's size and wealth and because the other fishing industries haven't been as well organized as the tuna industry. The arrival of the massive foreign fishing fleets off the Atlantic coast in the late 1960s and early 1970s, however, changed that. An indication of the increasing power of the other fisheries was the naming of representatives of several other fisheries to the U.S. advisory committee for the Law of the Sea Conference.[75]

Another indication of the friction between the various U.S. fisheries is the existence of several state laws that have added the complication of federal/state differences on fishing zones. A Massachusetts law of November 1971 authorizes the state's director of marine fisheries to regulate waters up to 200 miles offshore.[76] Rhode Island's general assembly considered a similar measure a short time later. Neither of these states considered the fact that they would be extending the state's claim to territorial waters. The motive for both states was to stimulate the federal government to take action on behalf of the commercial coastal fisheries. Massachusetts' director of marine fisheries has not acted under the terms of the law because he knows that the arrest of any boat beyond the three-mile limit would not be upheld by the courts.[77]

The 1966 legislation that added a nine-mile fishing zone contiguous to the three-mile U.S. territorial limit specified that it was neither extending nor diminishing existing state jurisdictions beyond the three-mile limit.[78] Both Texas and Florida claim jurisdiction over the nine miles based on prior legislation, the 1953 Submerged Lands Act, which divided jurisdiction over seabed resources between the state and federal governments. This became

problematical in 1971 when Florida's state coast guard
seized three Cuban shrimp boats and fined them for fishing in Florida's waters without a state fishing license.
The Supreme Court has agreed to rule on these conflicts
between federal and state jurisdiction.[79] It ruled in opposition to Alaska's arrest of Japanese fishing boats in
an attempt to regulate fishing in waters further than
three miles offshore.[80]

There are also conflicts between the tuna industry
and other interests in the United States. These competing
interest groups include the U.S. Navy, especially military
intelligence, the petroleum industry, the underwater mining industry, the transportation industry, the marine
sciences, and the conservation movements.[81] In general
the Navy has been the strongest supporter of the tuna industry's desire for minimum territorial seas. John Knauss
points out that traditionally the Navy prefers minimum
territorial seas off the coasts of other nations and extensions of the U.S. territorial waters for defense purposes. He believes that the changes in sophisticated
weaponry have divided the Navy into those who think in
the traditional terms of a surface navy, and those interested in intelligence operations who might prefer an extension of the limit.[82]

The most powerful and best-organized group of these
competing interests is the U.S. petroleum industry. Offshore wells now supply about 17 percent of the world's
petroleum; that figure is expected to double by the 1980s.
There are some 16,000 offshore wells in the United States
alone.[83] The position of the petroleum industry as formulated by the National Petroleum Council is a strong preference for national jurisdictions over the continental
shelf and continental slope for the United States and for
other nations. The oil industry, already accustomed to
dealing successfully with the known, separate national entities, wants to continue such a pattern, fearing an un-
known international regime. They believe that they would
have to have close cooperation from the coastal states
anyway in terms of supplies and pipelines.[84]

The current positions of the other interest groups
is not as clearly articulated. The mining industry supports some kind of international arrangement beyond national jurisdictions. The transportation industry is
very concerned about the tradition of "innocent passage."
Furthermore the conservation interest could become a more
important factor in shaping U.S. oceans policies. Canada's
100-mile pollution zone in the Arctic waters will be
watched carefully by U.S. conservationists.[85]

Finally, as was discussed in Chapter 3, the pressures of U.S. industries in Ecuador and Peru also complicate the sort of solution demanded by the tuna industry. Though the tuna industry still has the power to exercise linkage pressures on the U.S. government, there are competitive pressures being applied as well. The demands of the other fisheries are important rivals. The U.S. petroleum industry is pressuring from two angles: (1) it is making vigorous demands for diplomatic solution of the fisheries problem in order to protect its interest in the petroleum in Ecuador's Oriente province, and (2) it also demands extended national jurisdictions of the continental shelf and slopes. The role of other U.S. interests in Peru and Ecuador--whether in bananas or mining--also competes with the tuna industry. Finally, and by no means last in significance, the basic interest of U.S. policy in Latin America in general rejects a "get tough" position on the seizures as harmful to hemispheric goodwill. The claims and counterclaims of the various domestic pressure groups, and the goals and sensitivities of the various nations, mean that it will be difficult, perhaps nearly impossible, to agree on the least common denominator for establishing new rules for the uses of the oceans. The U.S. draft fisheries convention for the Law of the Sea Conference very neatly balances the wide variety of multiple U.S. interests in oceans policy. It remains to be seen whether other nations will perceive this sort of proposal as representing their own interests.

NOTES

1. J. L. Kask, "Tuna A World Resource," Occasional Paper No. 2 (Kingston, R.I.: The Law of the Sea Institute, May 1968), p. 22.
2. U.S. Senate, Committee on Commerce, Subcommittee on Oceans and Atmosphere, Hearings on Ocean Mammal Protection, 92d Cong., 2d sess., 1972, pt. I, p. 475.
3. Ibid.
4. Los Angeles Times, January 1, 1973, sec. 2.
5. Los Angeles Times, January 1, 1973, sec. 4.
6. U.S. Department of Commerce, Economic Development Administration, Feasibility Study: A Tuna Transshipment Plant in San Diego and Other Ocean-Oriented Facilities, May 1969, p. 8. This study was prepared by economic consultants Forbes, Stevenson, and Baldridge.

7. Thomas A. Pettit, "The Impact of Imports and Tariffs on the American Tuna Industry," The American Journal of Economics and Sociology 19, no. 3 (April 1960): 276-77.

8. Feasibility Study: A Tuna Transshipment Plant in San Diego and Other Ocean-Oriented Facilities, op. cit., p. 8.

9. U.S. House of Representatives, Committee on Merchant Marine and Fisheries, Subcommittee on Fisheries and Wildlife Conservation, Hearings on Illegal Seizures, 92d Cong., 1st sess., 1971, pp. 75-80.

10. Feasibility Study: A Tuna Transshipment Plant in San Diego and Other Ocean-Oriented Facilities, op. cit., pp. 77-82.

11. Interview conducted by the authors with August Fellando, General Manager, American Tunaboat Association, San Diego, California, September 6, 1972.

12. Los Angeles Times, February 7, 1971, sec. A.

13. Considerable literature exists on the economics of fisheries. See Expert Meeting on the Economic Effects of Fishery Regulation, Ottawa, 1961, Economic Effects of Fishery Regulation (working paper), ed. R. Hamlisch (Rome: FAO, 1962); James Crutchfield and Arnold Zellner, Economic Aspects of the Pacific Halibut Fishery, Fishery Industrial Research, April 1962, Department of the Interior, 1963, pp. 15-20; James Crutchfield, "The Marine Fisheries: A Problem in International Cooperation," American Economic Review (May 1964), pp. 207-18; and Francis T. Christy, Jr. and Anthony Scott, The Common Wealth in Ocean Fisheries: Some Problems of Growth and Economic Allocation (Baltimore: Johns Hopkins Press, 1965), pp. 221-30.

14. New York Times, March 22, 1971, p. 2.

15. Los Angeles Times, July 20, 1969, sec. H.

16. Food and Agriculture Organization, The State of the World's Fisheries (Rome: FAO, 1968), p. 34.

17. Interview with Fellando, op. cit.

18. Feasibility Study: A Tuna Transshipment Plant in San Diego and Other Ocean-Oriented Facilities, op. cit., p. 35.

19. "Todos tras los tunidos del mar peruano...menos los peruanos," Anuario de Pesca, 1968-1969, pp. 215-17.

20. Kask, op. cit., pp. 13-14.

21. Feasibility Study: A Tuna Transshipment Plant in San Diego and Other Ocean-Oriented Facilities, op. cit., p. 49.

22. Kask, op. cit., pp. 5-6.

23. Feasibility Study: A Tuna Transshipment Plant in San Diego and Other Ocean-Oriented Facilities, op. cit., pp. 65-72.

24. Ibid., pp. 5-16; and Los Angeles _Times_, July 20, 1969, sec. H.

25. Pettit, op. cit., p. 276.

26. Los Angeles _Times_, March 13, 1972, sec. H.

27. Pacific Island Development Commission, _An American Fisheries Opportunity in the Central and Western Pacific_, pp. 1-33.

28. Interview with Fellando, op. cit.

29. "El atun tropical y sus entrelones," _Anuario de Pesca, 1970-1971_, pp. 87-89.

30. _Latin America_ 5, no. 29 (July 16, 1971).

31. Los Angeles _Times_, March 4, 1971, sec. 2; New York _Times_, March 22, 1971, p. 2. See also _Hearings on Illegal Seizures_, op. cit., p. 178.

32. _Hearings on Illegal Seizures_, op. cit., pp. 37-39.

33. Interview with Fellando, op. cit.

34. Pettit, op. cit., p. 281.

35. _Feasibility Study: A Tuna Transshipment Plant in San Diego and Other Ocean-Oriented Facilities_, op. cit., pp. 28-29.

36. Los Angeles _Times_, February 18, 1972, sec. I.

37. New York _Times_, January 7, 1953, p. 85.

38. United States Tariff Commission, "Tuna Fish," May 1958.

39. Tariff Schedules of the United States Annotated (1972), Schedule I, Animal and Vegetable Products, Part 3--Fish and Shellfish.

40. Gabriel Almond, in _The Politics of Developing Areas_, ed. Gabriel Almond and James S. Coleman (Princeton: Princeton University Press, 1960), p. 34.

41. New York _Times_, January 30, 1971, p. 2.

42. _Hearings on Illegal Seizures_, op. cit., pp. 64-69.

43. Ibid., pp. 46-47.

44. Bernard C. Cohen, "Mass Communication and Foreign Policy," in _Domestic Sources of Foreign Policy_, ed. James N. Rosenau (New York: The Free Press, 1967), pp. 205-06.

45. _Hearings on Illegal Seizures_, op. cit., p. 105. See also the testimony by Assistant Secretary of State Charles A. Meyers, pp. 328-83.

46. Ibid., p. 5.

47. Ibid., pp. 336-40.

48. Fishermen's Protective Act of 1954, 22 U.S.C.: 1971-76 (1964).

49. Fishermen's Protective Act of 1967, P.L. No. 90-482, 82 Stat. 729 (1968), 22 U.S.C.: 1971-77.

50. P.L. 92-950.

51. _The Fish Boat_ 16, no. 1 (January 1971): 15.

52. <u>Hearings on Illegal Seizures</u>, op. cit., pp. 331-40. See also U.S. Senate, Committee on Commerce, Subcommittee on Oceans and Atmosphere, <u>Hearings on Fishery Legislation</u>, 92d Cong., 1st sess., 1971, pp. 48-50.

53. P.L. 89-171, 79 Stat. 660 (1965).

54. P.L. 90-224, 81 Stat. 729 (1967).

55. P.L. 90-629, 82 Stat. 1320 (1968).

56. <u>Hearings on Illegal Seizures</u>, op. cit., p. 334.

57. P.L. 92-242, Title I, Sec. 113.

58. New York <u>Times</u>, March 4, 1972, p. 28.

59. H.R. 10607 (1969). Hearings were planned for this proposed legislation but were never held, even though testimony was prepared for the prospective hearings by some groups, including the American Tunaboat Association and Representative Pelly.

60. <u>Congressional Record</u> 118, no. 11 (February 11, 1972), H469-75; P.L. 92-246.

61. <u>Hearings on Fishery Legislation</u>, op. cit., pp. 45-50.

62. P.L. 92-569, October 26, 1972.

63. <u>Hearings on Fishery Legislation</u>, op. cit., pp. 2-5, 116-18.

64. Los Angeles <u>Times</u>, October 20, 1972, sec. I.

65. U.S. House of Representatives, Committee on Merchant Marine and Fisheries, Subcommittee on Fisheries and Wildlife Conservation, <u>Hearings on Marine Mammals</u>, 92d Cong., 1st sess., 1971, pp. 344-55.

66. <u>Hearings on Ocean Mammal Protection</u>, pt. I, pp. 475-92.

67. "Marine Mammal Act of 1972," P.L. 92-522, October 21, 1972.

68. New York <u>Times</u>, April 9, 1972, sec. 4, and May 30, 1972, p. 36.

69. Charles T. Goodsell, "Diplomatic Protection of U.S. Business in Peru," in <u>U.S. Foreign Policy in Peru</u>, ed. Daniel A. Sharp (Austin: University of Texas Press, 1972), pp. 244-46.

70. U.S. House of Representatives, Committee on Merchant Marine and Fisheries, "Establishing a Contiguous Fisheries Zone Beyond the Territorial Sea of the United States," Report No. 2086, 89th Cong., 2d sess., 1966.

71. New York <u>Times</u>, March 14, 1972, p. 57.

72. New York <u>Times</u>, June 5, 1971, p. 56.

73. <u>Fishing Gazette</u> 89, no. 3 (March 1972): 24.

74. Interview with Fellando; Los Angeles <u>Times</u>, October 15, 1972, sec. C.

75. Los Angeles _Times_, October 15, 1972, sec. C.
This does not mean that the California-based tuna industry
is without representation. It is, in fact, well repre-
sented on the Fisheries Subcommittee of the Advisory Com-
mittee on the Law of the Sea, with the following members:
Charles R. Carry, executive director of the Tuna Research
Foundation, Inc.; August Fellando, general manager of the
American Tunaboat Association; and John J. Royal, secretary-
treasurer of Fishermen and Allied Workers' Union, Local 33,
I.L.W., San Pedro, California.

76. _Christian Science Monitor_, November 22, 1971,
p. 20.

77. _The Fish Boat_ 17, no. 2 (February 1972): 11;
and 17, no. 4 (April 1972): 21.

78. P.L. 89-658; 80 Stat. 908.

79. _Wall Street Journal_, March 31, 1972, p. 4.

80. Arctic Maid Fisheries, Inc. et al. v. State of
Alaska, _International Legal Materials_ 2 (1963): 524-26.
See also the letter of Secretary of State Dean Rusk that
follows on pp. 528-29.

81. John A. Knauss, "Factors Influencing a U.S.
Position in a Future Law of the Sea Conference," Occa-
sional Paper No. 10 (Kingston, R.I.: The Law of the Sea
Institute, February 1969).

82. Ibid., pp. 2-5.

83. Ibid., p. 12.

84. Robert L. Friedheim, "Understanding the Debate
on Ocean Resources," Occasional Paper No. 1 (Kingston,
R.I.: The Law of the Sea Institute, February 1969), pp.
16-17.

85. Knauss, op. cit., pp. 15-16.

CHAPTER

6

CONCLUSIONS

The problems of Latin American fisheries and inter-
American relations are complex, multifaceted, and interrelated. They are both domestic and international situa-
tions encompassing scientific, economic, and political
considerations. They are also instructive about the fine
lines of distinction between the dependency, independence,
and interdependence of nations. Sometimes the achievement
of one kind of independence brings with it another sort of
dependence. For example Peru's achievement of greater
economic independence from the domination of her economy
by minerals exports through developing her fishmeal industry has brought with it dependence on both the world price
of fishmeal as well as the steady availability of anchovies
in the Humboldt Current. Peru cannot completely control
either of these factors. The same may be true of political
dependence and independence as well. The shucking of Latin
America's traditional dependence on the United States in
foreign policy may bring with it a new dependence on another nation or group of nations. On this subject, where
fluctuations of national attitude are as apparent as fluctuations in the fishing harvest, and where change itself
may be the only constant, it is risky to pronounce abso-
lute conclusions. Having stated this caveat, we think
this study substantiates the following conclusions:

1. The problems of Latin American fisheries and
inter-American relations display interrelationships between domestic and international politics. The territorial waters dispute has had an impact on the domestic
politics of all the nations involved. Both Latin American
and U.S. politicians have used the claims-seizure dispute
to build their own reputations as hard-liners. The claimants have discovered the 200-mile claim as a safe tactic

for exploiting the powerful current of Yankeephobia without damaging any major, or perhaps minor, sector of their
political economy. For this reason even nations lacking
the abundance of the Humboldt Current have responded
eagerly to the example of the CEP claims.

The reverse is also true--domestic politics also has
influenced the foreign policies in the claims dispute.
Perhaps this is shown most clearly in the zealous efforts
of the U.S. tuna industry to achieve a legislative remedy
for the seizures. In Latin America domestic pressures,
including those applied by the hemisphere's international
lawyers, the Latin American navies, and the Peruvian fishmeal industry, have influenced foreign policy.

Furthermore it is also clear that the entire international arena has affected the claims dispute. For example less developed nations increasingly are defining
"freedom of the seas" to mean unlimited plunder of the
sea's resources by the developed maritime nations. The
international race for tuna, stimulated by high market
values, has prompted some governments to subsidize the
construction of large tuna fleets. These are economic
policy decisions with important foreign policy ramifications. The growing concern for species conservation and
other general ecological considerations, as well as the
multipolar world competition for friends, allies, and
trade partners, also illustrate the impact of the international arena on particular foreign policies.

2. Fisheries, because they operate on the threshold
of a nation's foreign policy, much like multinational
corporations, are able to influence both domestic and
foreign policy. Peru's fishmeal oligarchs, because of
the external nature of their trade, were able to press
for the devaluation of the Peruvian currency in 1967.
The U.S. tuna industry pressured successfully for a series
of retaliatory laws designed to punish and prevent
seizures.

3. National policies designed to protect certain national interests also can damage other national interests.
The nonrecognition of the 200-mile claim by the United
States, even though it met the demands of the tuna industry and the Pentagon, has been a 20-year irritant hamper-
ing good hemispheric relations. There are growing counter-
pressures on the U.S. government to avoid policies that
may threaten the U.S. investments in Latin American petroleum, agriculture, and mining. And to the dismay of the
tuna industry there is serious defection from the ranks
of U.S. fisheries on U.S. policy toward its own exclusive

fishing zone. The tuna industry can no longer presume to
represent all U.S. fisheries in opposing unilateral extensions of fishing zones. Other fisheries have filled that
vacuum and are pressuring for a U.S. extension to protect
its offshore resources from foreign fleets.

4. A pressure group with effective access to the nation's policy-makers may be unable to achieve a solution
satisfactory to it in the long run. The Peruvian junta
has reduced the impact of the fishmeal oligarchs most recently by nationalizing the entire industry. The U.S.
tuna industry, even though it had effective access to Congress, the U.S. public, and occasionally to the administration, has been disappointed by the continuation of seizures
and the increasingly punitive fines. It may have access to
U.S. policy-makers, but it lacks effective access to the
decision-makers of the claimant nations. There are also
other powerful domestic interests working at cross-purposes
with the tuna industry. It also seems likely that the tuna
industry itself may become more divided, especially if the
canneries expand their operations further in Latin America.

5. The passage of time has not healed the inter-
American fisheries dispute. In fact both the number and
respectability of the offshore claims have increased with
the passage of time. And as it has become apparent that
the maritime nations are unwilling or unable to force retraction of the claims, the attractiveness of using an extension to flaunt the growth of independence from the traditional role expected of Latin American nations has increased the number of claimants and potential claimants.
The primary deterrent to those Latin American nations that
have not extended their claims has been their fears of
conflicting claims with their immediate neighbors rather
than the fear of retaliation from the maritime nations.
In sum the passage of time has increased the attractiveness of the extension claims, even with some of the U.S.
fishing industries.

6. It is uncertain at this time whether the Law of
the Sea Conference will be able to achieve a universally
acceptable international treaty regulating the multiple
uses of the oceans. Probably most claimants would be
pleased to have a 200-mile economic zone sanctioned by
international treaty; even Peru might accept this sort of
definition. It now appears that the patrimonial sea distinction favored by Venezuela and other nations is the
sort of definition of the claim that most claimants will
accept. It seems quite unlikely that they will relinquish
the 200-mile terminology; such terminology is much too

important a symbol of increased Latin American independence.
The U.S. draft fisheries convention, based on the principle
of species' life cycles rather than territorial distance,
is certainly the most logical way to insure species conservation. Such a proposal may be regarded with considerable
suspicion, however, because it also appears to protect a
good many U.S. fishing interests: coastal fishing, Alaskan
salmon, and the traditional distant-water industries of
shrimp and tuna--at least insofar as the coastal nations'
capacity to harvest the resources continues to be limited.
Despite the unpredictability of the conference's outcome,
however, so much effort and delicate bargaining has gone
into the preparations for the conference that we are hopeful that the 1974 conference will be able to conclude with
more than the agreement to disagree that characterized the
preceding Law of the Sea Conferences.

ABOUT THE AUTHORS

Both Bobbie Braly Smetherman and Robert M. Smetherman are currently teaching at California State University, Fresno. She is Coordinator of Women's Studies and an Instructor in Political Science. He is Professor of History and is also the President-Elect of the Pacific Coast Council for Latin American Studies.

In the past Bobbie Smetherman taught at New York Institute of Technology and Robert Smetherman taught at Post College, Long Island University. The authors have been interested in several aspects of inter-American relations since their doctoral studies were completed at Claremont Graduate School.

In their collaborative research the Drs. Smetherman have travelled throughout Latin America and Central America. Jointly they have written several articles on various aspects of inter-American relations, including U.S. foreign aid to Latin America, as well as the 200-mile claim and seizures of fishing boats. They are continuing on these and other aspects of inter-American relations. Currently their special area of emphasis is on developing frictions between the United States and Mexico, especially over fisheries and territorial claims.

OCEAN SPACE RIGHTS: Developing
U.S. Policy
                    Lawrence Juda

THE INTERNATIONAL POLITICS OF
MARINE POLLUTION CONTROL
                    Robert A. Shinn

MULTILATERAL SANCTIONS IN INTERNATIONAL
LAW: A Comparative Analysis
                    C. Lloyd Brown-John